"Rakoff knows the incantatory power of a story well-told, the art of keeping words aloft like the bubbles in a champagne flute. He possesses the crackling wit of a '30s screwball comedy ingénue, a vocabulary that is a treasure chest of mots justes, impressive but most times not too showy for everyday wear." —*Los Angeles Times*

"Rakoff has a self-awareness that could be re-created only by a team of geneticists working in a lab. The conviction with which he writes is, at the risk of blowing his jacket, uplifting." —*The New York Times*

"Full of wit." —*Fresh Air* (NPR)

"Rakoff can issue a withering snark with the best of them. But once his rapier wit has sliced the buttons off his target's clothing, revealing the quivering, vulnerable mass within, his fundamental sense of decency gets the best of him." —*Salon*

"*Half Empty* balances its darker aspects with wickedly amusing takes on a variety of subjects." —*The Toronto Star*

"Looking like a pug and sounding like the love child of Dorothy Parker, Oscar Wilde and *All About Eve*'s Addison DeWitt, he is smug, insufferable and self-infatuated to a fare-thee-well. He's magnificent." —*The Atlanta Journal-Constitution*

"If you love the personal essay, you'll love David Rakoff's musings." —*The Baltimore Sun*

"Rakoff is so keenly observant and dead-on with his criticism, you get the impression most of our eyes would cross and cartoon birds fly above our heads before we could make it halfway to the elegant, smart conclusions he draws. . . . A writerly collection to make giddy even the most erudite lover of words. An undisputed KO for negative thinking."

—*Booklist*

"It is not unusual to find a humorist that is funny. But it is unusual to find a humorist that is smart and wry and sensitive as well. We find all that in David Rakoff."

—*The Post & Courier* (Charleston)

"Hucksters and money-grubbing visionaries will always be with us. With any luck we will also have writers like Rakoff to whack them upside their swollen, empty heads."

—*Minneapolis Star Tribune*

"Rakoff manages to make pessimism sexy. . . . While Rakoff seems to revel in his role as a modern-day Thomas Hobbes, it's evident that he remains responsible in his critique, never trouncing a subject without provocation while simultaneously opening the reader's eyes to everyday lunacy."

—*Kirkus Reviews*

DAVID RAKOFF

Half Empty

David Rakoff is the author of the books *Fraud* and *Don't Get Too Comfortable*. A two-time recipient of the Lambda Literary Award, he is a regular contributor to Public Radio International's *This American Life*. His writing has appeared in the *New York Times*, *Newsweek*, *Wired*, *Salon*, *GQ*, *Outside*, *Gourmet*, *Vogue*, *Slate*, *Harper's Bazaar*, and the *New York Observer*, among other publications, and has been included in *Da Capo's Best Music Writing*, *The Best American Travel Writing*, as well as *The Best American Non-Required Reading*. He can be seen in the movies *Capote* (fleetingly), *Strangers with Candy* (fleetingly; mutely), and, most recently, he adapted the screenplay for and starred in Joachim Back's film *The New Tenants*, which won the 2010 Oscar for Best Live Action Short.

Also by David Rakoff

Fraud
Don't Get Too Comfortable

Half Empty

David Rakoff

Anchor Books
A Division of Random House, Inc.
New York

FIRST ANCHOR BOOKS EDITION, SEPTEMBER 2011

Portions of this work previously appeared in slightly different form in *Gourmet, The New York Times, Nextbook,* and *Spin.*

The Library of Congress cataloged the Doubleday edition as follows:
Rakoff, David.
Half empty / David Rakoff.—1st ed.
p. cm.
1. American wit and humor. I. Title.
PN6165.R35 2010
814'.6—dc22   2010007753

Anchor ISBN: 978-0-7679-2905-9

Book design by Michael Collica

www.anchorbooks.com

Printed in the United States of America
10 9 8 7 6 5 4 3 2 1

For
Patty Marx, Kent Sepkowitz,
and Bill Thomas

If there was nothing to regret,
there was nothing to desire.

—Vera Pavlova

Contents

Half
Empty

The Bleak Shall Inherit

We were so happy. It was miserable.

Although it was briefly marvelous and strange to see a car parked outside an office, the wide hallway used like a street, many stories above the city.

The millennium had turned. The planes had not fallen from the sky, the trains had not careened off the tracks. Neither had the heart monitors, prenatal incubators, nor the iron lungs reset themselves to some suicidal zero hour to self-destruct in a lethal *kablooey* of Y2K shrapnel, as feared. And most important, the ATMs continued to dispense money, and what money it was.

I was off to see some of it. Like Edith Wharton's Gilded Age Buccaneers, when titled but cash-poor Europeans joined in wedlock with wealthy American girls in the market for pedigree, there were mutually abusive marriages popping up all over the city between un-moneyed creatives with ethereal Web-based schemes and the financiers who, desperate to get in on the action, bankrolled them. The Internet at that point was still newish and completely uncharted territory, to me, at least. I had walked away from a job at what would undoubtedly have been the wildly lucrative ground floor (1986, Tokyo) because it had seemed so boring, given my aggressive lack of interest in technology or machines, unless they make food. Almost fifteen years later, I was no more curious nor convinced, but now found myself at numerous parties for start-ups, my comprehension of which extended no further than the free snacks and drinks, and the perfume of money-scented elation in the air. The workings of "new media" remained entirely murky, and I a baffled hypocrite, scarfing down another beggar's purse with crème fraîche (flecked with just enough beads of caviar to get credit), pausing in my chewing only long enough to mutter "It'll never last." It was becoming increasingly difficult to fancy myself the guilelessly astute child at the procession who points out the emperor's nakedness as acquaintances were suddenly becoming millionaires on paper and legions of twenty-one-year-olds were securing lucrative and rewarding positions as "content providers" instead of answering phones for a living, as I had at that age. Brilliant success was all around.

So, so happy.

The surly Russian janitor (seemingly the only other New Yorker in a bad mood) rode me up in his dusty elevator in the vast deco building in the West Twenties, which was now home to cyber and design concerns that gravitated to its raw spaces and industrial cachet. The kind of place where the freight car and the corridors are both wide enough that you'd never have to get out of your Lexus until you'd parked it on the fourteenth floor.

Book publishing is always portrayed as *teddibly* genteel and literary: hunter-green walls, morocco-bound volumes, and some old codger in a waistcoat going on about dear Max Perkins. Worlds away from the reality of dropped-ceiling offices with seas of cubicles and mail-cart-scarred walls. But the Internet companies were coevolving with the fictionalized idealization of themselves. The way they looked in the movies was also how they looked in real life, much like real-life mobsters who now behave like the characters in the *Godfather* films.

The large industrial casement windows were masculine with grime, looking out over the rail yards on the open sky of West Side Manhattan. The content providers sat side by side at long metal trestle tables—the kind they use in morgues—providing content, the transparent turquoise bubbles of their iMacs shining like insect eyes. It was a painfully hip dystopia, some Orwellian Ministry of Malign Intent whose sheer stylishness made it a pleasure to be a chic and soulless drone; one's personal freedoms happily abrogated for a Hugo Boss jumpsuit.

I was there to interview the founders of a site that was to be the one stop where members of the media might log on to read about themselves and the latest magazine-world gossip, schadenfreude-laden items about hefty book advances and who was seen lunching at Michael's, etc. I will stipulate to a certain degree of prejudicial thinking before I even walked in. I expected a bunch of aphoristic, McLuhan-lite bushwa, something to justify the house-of-cards business model. But as a reporter, I was their target audience as well as a colleague. I was unprepared to be spoken to like an investor, as if I, too, were some venture capitalist who goes goggled-eyed and compliant at the mere mention of anything nonnumerical. I was being lubed up with snake oil, listening to a bunch of pronouncements that sounded definitive and guru-like on the surface but which upon examination seemed just plain old wrong.

"What makes a story really good and *Webby*," said one, "is, say, we post an item on David Geffen on a Monday, and then one of Geffen's people calls us to correct it, we can have a whole new version up by Tuesday." This was typical Dawn of the New Millennium denigration of print, which always seemed to lead to the faulty logic that it was not just the delivery system that was outmoded but such underlying practices as authoritative voice and credibility, fact-checking, editing, and impartiality that needed throwing out, too. It was a stance they both seemed a little old for, frankly, like watching a couple of forty-five-year-olds in backward baseball caps on skateboards. In the future, it seems, we would all take our editorial marching orders from the powerful subjects of our stories and it would be good (*Right you are, Mr. Geffen!*). It was a challenge to sit there and be told that caring about such things as journalistic independence or the desire to keep money's influence at even a show of remove meant one was clinging to old beliefs, a fossil in the making. Now that everything and everyone was palliated by the never-ending flow of revenue, there was no need to get exercised about such things, or about anything, really.

"We basically take John Seabrook's view that what you have is more important than what you believe. Whether you drive a Cadillac says more about you than if you're a Democrat or a Republican," said one, invoking a (print) journalist from *The New Yorker*.

Added the other: "That you watched *The Sopranos* last night is more important than who you voted for."

They weren't saying anything terribly incendiary. It's not like they were proposing tattooing people who have HIV the way odious William F. Buckley did (I'm sorry, I mean brilliant and courtly, such manners, and what a *vocabulary*! Nazi . . .). But we had just been through an electoral experience that had been bruising, to say the least. Who one voted for had almost never seemed more important, and they were saying it all so blithely. I felt like a wife who has caught her tobacco-and-gin-scented husband smeared in lipstick, a pair of silk panties sticking out of his jacket pocket, home after an unexplained three-day absence, listening to his giggling, sloppily improbable, and casually delivered alibi and being expected to swallow it while chuckling along.

We were silent for a moment, the only sound the keyboard tappings of the hipster minions. I finally managed to say, "I've just experienced the death of hope."

We all three laughed: me, in despair; them, all the way to the bank. Said one of them, "No, David. We are the very opposite. This is the *birth* of hope!"

Down in the rattling freight elevator. I couldn't face going home just then, where I would have to immediately relive this conversation by transcribing my tape. I turned right out of the building, crossed Eleventh Avenue, and sat on a concrete barrier facing the river. The cynicism of the interview, the lack of belief coupled with the enthusiastic tone in which the bullshit was being slung, the raiding-the-granaries greed dressed up in the cheap drag of some hollow dream of a Bright New Day of it all. The Hudson bleared and wobbled before my eyes, which were swimming with furious tears. I wasn't angry to the point of almost crying because they were wrong but because they were right.

It might seem a bit much to pin the woes of the age on the fairly modest landgrab of the two men I had just interviewed, but they were symptomatic of something. In blithe defiance of some very real evidence out there that we still had reason for some very real concern, rampant optimism, fueled by money and a maddening fingers-in-the-ears-*can't-hear-you-lalala* denial, was now carrying the day. There seemed no longer to be any room in the discourse for anything but the sunniest outlook.

Contrarianism needed restoring to its rightful stature as loyal opposition and so I found myself, some four months later, on my way to Wellesley College to interview a psychologist named Julie Norem.

Norem's book, *The Positive Power of Negative Thinking*, was about to come out and the same magazine, for whom I had shed my Hudson River tears, was now sending me to document this emotional market correction. It was one I welcomed, and judging from the title, one my editors were hoping—as editors must—would present as a forceful linchpin theory, a reductive cudgel of a book that would advocate wholesale crankiness, a call to arms that we all rain on each other's parades, piss in one another's cereal, kick puppies, and smack babies.

As the schoolgirl said to the vicar, it was a lot less meaty up close. The book was terrifically smart and well-wrought, but Norem had emphatically not written a book against happiness. Her research dealt with a specific kind of anxiety-management technique known as "defensive pessimism." Defensive pessimism is related to dispositional pessimism—that clinical, Eeyore-like negativity—but it is, at most, a first cousin. One who is kickier and more fun to be around; played by the same actress but with her glasses off, a different hairstyle, and a "visiting for the summer from swinging London" accent.

Both dispositional and defensive pessimists face life with that same negative prediction: "This [insert impending experience, encounter, endeavor here] will be a disaster." But where the dispositional pessimist sees that gloomy picture as a verdict and pretext to return to or simply remain in bed, the defensive pessimist uses it as the first of a three-part process: 1) the a priori lowered expectations (the previously mentioned presentiment of disaster) are followed by 2) a detailed breakdown of the situation (the "this will suck *because* . . ." stage), wherein one envisions the specific ways in which the calamity will take shape. A worst-case scenario painted in as much detail as possible. The process culminates in 3) coming up with the various responses and remedies to each possible misstep along the way ("I will arrive early and make sure the microphone cord is taped down," "I'll have my bear spray in my hand before I leave the cabin," "I'll put the Xanax under my tongue forty minutes before the party and pretend not to remember his name when I see him," etc.). A sea of troubles, opposed and ended, one nigglesome wave at a time. Defensive pessimism is about sweating the small stuff, being prepared for contingencies like some neurotic Jewish Boy Scout, and in so doing, not letting oneself be crippled by fear. Where a strategic optimist might approach a gathering rainstorm with a smile as his umbrella, the defensive pessimist, all too acquainted with this world of pitfall and precipitation, is far more likely to use, well, an umbrella.

This mental preparation is just an alternate means of coping with a world where—in the pessimist's view of reality—there is often little difference between "worst possible outcome" and "outcome." A world seen as worse than it actually is. Through such eyes, the optimist looks hopelessly naïve. As Prohibition-era newspaperman Don Marquis put it in 1927, another age when unwarranted exuberance and eye-off-the-ball hubris led to its own inevitable disaster, "an optimist is a guy that has never had much experience." But Norem explains that optimists, too, have their own mental strategies of navigating a world that seems far better than it is in reality. They need to sustain a cognitive conundrum known as "ironic processing," a willful "whatever you do, don't think about it" ignorance, blind to even the possibility of negative outcome. In a study where subjects were made to play darts, defensive pessimists who were robbed of their time for mental rehearsal and instead made to relax, free of thought, were thrown off their game. Conversely, optimists also found their anxieties increase and their performances suffer by being made to contemplate strategy and contingency before taking aim.

It might seem that the twain shall never meet and at best one might achieve some grudging mutual understanding, but cognition and its styles exist on a continuum. Pessimists are born, true, but they also can be made. Two social psychologists out of Cornell named Justin Kruger and David Dunning bore this out to a degree in a study where they asked subjects to assess their skill levels in a number of areas, on which they would be tested. What they found was that those who scored lowest had rated themselves highest. The same held true in reverse: high-scoring subjects had underestimated their skills and how well they compared with others. When the over-raters received instruction, namely, when they became intrinsically more skilled than before, their sense of their own competence diminished. Experience had shown them how much more there was to learn, how far they still had to go, and their self-assessments reflected this.

Given all of this—that one need but point out the ways in which we were royally screwed to have the scales fall from people's eyes—how was it possible for Norem's book *not* to be the antidote to all the unchecked and unearned exuberance of the age? This volume would finally wake folks up, I thought. The bleak would inherit the earth!

(I had chosen that moment, it seems, to forget yet again my unique incapacity for identifying trends. If I think something is going to happen, it invariably results in the very opposite non-event. Conversely, if I smell doom, there will be nothing but brilliant success. My finger is securely off the pulse. Walking away from the Internet in 1986 is just one instance in an illustrious résumé of bad calls.

In 1982, as a freshman in college, during a brief and ultimately fruitless attempt at inhabiting my own skin, I went one evening to Danceteria, a club in downtown Manhattan. I didn't drink at the time, so there was nothing to buffer the noise, the dark, the crowded stairwells, the too-long wait for both the coat check and the urinals, and *especially* that evening's entertainment: a whiny, nasal girl in torn lace and rubber-gasket bracelets who bopped around to an over-synthesized and generic backbeat.

"Well, *she's* lousy," I thought to myself, happily envisioning my departure from this throbbing club, my subway ride uptown to my dorm room and bed, and this girl's return to the obscurity whence she sprung. The world, however, had different plans for Madonna. *"Hey David, have you seen that fellow in the market-place inveighing against the Pharisees and the money-changers? You know, the one who calls himself the Son of God?" "That idiot? He'll burn off like so much morning fog, mark my words . . ."*

Bet against me, and I will make you rich. I am the un-canary in the mine shaft. (*Gas? I don't smell no gas!*)

Norem herself was less absolute about the book's chances at effecting any wholesale paradigm shift in the public psyche. She was advocating negative thinking only to the extent that if that was the way your mind already worked, then you ought not to be seen as counterproductive or in need of an immediate attitude adjustment. She was not calling for a glorious new epoch of sad-sack sobriety. All Norem was saying was that there should be room enough at the table for a greater spectrum of feeling. That one's cognitive style was ultimately as value neutral as the color of one's hair, even though pessimism might very well feel less pleasurable than optimism (although try telling that to the adolescent girl voluptuously bathing in that exquisite sea of heartbreak as she is locked in her bedroom listening to music and sketching portraits of limpid-eyed, tear-shedding soulful girls with lank hair and guitars, all while hating her parents). Pointing out that negative emotions are in no way lesser than their citrus-colored counterparts, just different, might seem incredibly basic, but it was an absolutely revolutionary statement.

That said, *The Positive Power of Negative Thinking* had a very narrow focus, one almost completely free of bombast or polemic. What it most definitely was *not*, for example, was a takedown of the reigning school of the prevailing culture, the positive psychology movement. This deeply funded but loosely organized group of clinicians and researchers was dedicated to returning the field of psychology to its original three missions of curing mental illness, making the lives of all people more fulfilling, and fostering human talent. According to the group's founder, Dr. Martin Seligman, the author of such books as *Learned Optimism* and *The Optimistic Child*, we had lost sight of all but the first objective since World War II, concentrating too much on the sick and unhappy and leaving the relatively well and potentially excellent among us to fend for themselves.

"We became a victimology . . . Psychology is not just the study of weakness and damage, it is also the study of strength and virtue," Seligman wrote in his monthly column for the *APA Monitor* in 1989, the year he served as president of the American Psychological Association. We have managed to help people go from negative five to zero, he says, but if you're looking to get up into the positive integers, mental health–wise, you're on your own. The happy and gifted among us were essentially taking their marching orders from the vast, gray masses of the unhappy bottom and middle. The movement was an attempt to address this imbalance.

Seligman refers to that which is solely concerned with disease and disorder as "remedial psychology." "How has it happened that the social sciences view the human strengths and virtues— altruism, courage, honesty, duty, joy, health, responsibility, and good cheer—as derivative, defensive, or downright illusions, while weakness and negative motivations—anxiety, lust, selfishness, paranoia, anger, disorder, and sadness—are viewed as authentic?" he asks.

While Norem had no quarrel with the movement's desire to study all human emotion and not just the troubled end of the spectrum, she did have issues with its premise. "Any movement should only have the status of a scientific movement if the outcomes of research, what is going to be proclaimed to be adaptive or healthy, are not preordained." It's far easier to swallow a mouthful of honey than one of curry powder, but one doesn't then judge the former an elixir and the latter poison. Positive feelings may redound to positive outcomes, but it isn't a given, despite what we are told, and we *are* told, all the time and in countless ways. "The consequences are not inherent in the emotion itself. It is a sloppy assumption that hedonically positive emotion is related to positive outcomes. Positive emotions *may*, of course, relate to good things, but there is no necessary relationship. Pride, for example, is positive in that it feels good. It may lead people to work hard or behave well, but it may also lead them to treat others shabbily. Embarrassment is negative because nobody likes how it feels, and it can have negative consequences, but it can also be a powerfully pro-social emotion [hello, Canada!]. The consequences are not inherent in the emotion itself."

Norem is absolutely right. It is the false equation of what *feels* good with what *is* good that rankles. Self-esteem might seem an unimpeachably positive state, but you don't have to sit through an endless children's talent show (is there any other kind?) to know that it has reached unhealthy and epidemic proportions in this country.

More than the shaky corollaries, though, it was the prickling, Ayn Rand–ish sensation that troubled me. Seligman wrote of a

Manhattan Project of sorts being set up to explore how to foster personal strength and civic virtue, returning our society to the greatness of ages past: the democracy of Athens; the honor, discipline, and duty of Victorian England; the pursuit of beauty that was classical Florence. "My vision," he writes, "is that social science will finally see beyond the remedial and escape from the muckraking that has claimed it, that social science will become a positive force for understanding and promoting the highest qualities of civic and personal life."

I'll leave the glories of ancient Athens's slave class, Victorian England's debtors' prisons (and the rampant syphilis among the child prostitutes resulting from just such parental incarcerations), and the grinding poverty of those Florentines not fortunate enough to be Medicis up to the historians. A return to notions of discipline and civic virtue would be welcome, God knows, but I'm not convinced that social scientists are muckrakers conducting more studies about widespread income disparity, infant mortality, or suicide rates than they are about more positive human endeavors (if, in fact, they are) simply because they find them more "authentic," or because of some kind of if-it-bleeds-it-leads sensationalism, or worse yet—in classic blaming the thermometer for the temperature—that scrutinizing such problems somehow exacerbates their power and unpleasant effect on the rest of us. It must be a vestigial race memory of the maple-scented egalitarianism of my Canadian upbringing that makes me find it unattractively greedy for the essentially satisfied to demand still greater satisfaction.

But more than any abstemious impulse to ration out help to those who barely need it, it's the false division that so repels me. The vision of these warring constituencies—the gloomy hordes, sucking up all available time and resources from the shiny, happy, excellent few. I keep flashing back to what it says

14

in the *Inferno:* "There is no greater pain than to remember happiness in the midst of one's misery." There will be peaks of great joy from which to crow and vales of tears out of which to climb. When and why they will happen, no one can say, but they will happen. To all of us. We will all go back and forth from one to the other countless times during a lifetime. This is not some call to bipartisanship between inimical sides. The Happy and the Sad are the same population.

There is a question that frequently runs through the reporter's mind when he is sent on assignment and the story as initially envisioned is failing to bear fruit, and that question is this: "Am I fucked?" It was ricocheting through my brain as I, tape recorder in hand, walked the leafy quads of Wellesley with Julie Norem, and the answer that was pinging back was a qualified yes. Norem's conclusions were too measured, her argument too subtle for an easily digestible and zeitgeisty magazine piece.

But it was not the subtlety of Norem's argument that was in the way as much as I myself. A therapy junkie I know is fond of parroting the adage: "All research is Me-search." Even though I had read *The Positive Power of Negative Thinking* very carefully before arriving, I had come up to Massachusetts thinking, hoping, that Norem had actually written a book not about anxiety but about sadness. Specifically, *my* sadness—highly unlikely as we had only just met that very day.

Anxiety and sadness often occur at the same time. Psychological assessments for sadness often look for an anxiety component, but they are absolutely separate. One can be anxious *and* happy, for example (an incomprehensible combination to my mind, like Jewish Republicans). I couldn't for the life of me tease the anxious and sad strands apart, so I spent a good portion of the day asking poor Julie Norem to once more explain the difference to me. She was doubtless very glad to drop me off at the Amtrak station six hours later.

My confusion was making me stupid in other ways, too. On the train back, I realized that I had allowed the cassette to auto-reverse on itself over and over, all day long, like a weaver's shuttle. I had lost many of the hours and hours of questions and answers in a magnetic pentimento. Even as I sat there in the Quiet Car, my hand covering my mouth in wonder at my "yes I am indeed fucked . . . so very, very fucked" stupidity, I was not hugely surprised at this small act of self-sabotage: I didn't want to write this piece.

So I didn't.

In the three weeks leading up to the due date, I did no writing at all, aside from my self-pitying, stultifying diary, whose entries all began "T minus X days," referring to the twentieth, when I would have to call my editor and tell her that I had failed, without even the necessary pages of twaddle I'd need to qualify for a kill fee. I was Penelope at her loom, filling my time with busywork. I woke each day at the crack and, when it seemed appropriate, I would pick up the phone and begin that day's interviews with other psychologists, all purportedly in the name of re(me)search.

I spoke to James Pennebaker, the chair of the Department of Psychology at the University of Texas in Austin, who worked with survivors of traumatic experiences. He found that if patients wrote, talked about, or articulately confronted what they had gone through, as opposed to suppressing the feelings, they showed marked improvements in physical health, immune function, and other markers. In another study he conducted in 1989 with David Watson, they found that even the kvetchiest patients, those with the least-positive attitudes, who complained most about their symptoms, turned out to be no objectively sicker than those with low negative affect. It was nice to find out, then, that if one is characterologically incapable of *not* being a total fuckface, science has not shown you will die any sooner. People might just be gladder when you eventually do.

David Lykken conducted the Minnesota Study of Twins (*not* the baseball team; think Doublemint, or Romulus and Remus), collecting data from hundreds of pairs of identical and fraternal twins for years, measuring their subjective well-being (SWB)— their self-reported happiness—and found that "the effects on current SWB of both positive and negative life events are largely gone after just three months and undetectable after six . . . Most people will have adapted back to their genetically determined set-point." Lykken found this to be the case across the board among his subjects, regardless of economic, racial, ethnic, gender, or other circumstantial factors. So if you win the lottery or have your limbs lopped off by an oncoming train, within 180 days, you'll be back to your old self, which is very good—or bad—to know.

Many scientists have challenged Lykken's results, and the media has misinterpreted his findings, often conflating the malleable and potential notion of heritability with the genetic verdict of heredity. Even Lykken himself contends that one mustn't use one's set-point as a pretext for resigning oneself to one's DNA.

"After we published that study, I said something like 'trying to be happier is like trying to be taller,' and I regretted that as soon as I saw it in print," said Lykken on the phone. "It was a smart-aleck comment and in fact I wrote a book to contradict it . . . one can manage to bounce along above one's set-point, if you play your cards right and if you realize that the striving for winning the lottery or the big goals is not the solution unless working to get there is in itself gratifying . . . the important thing is that nature has equipped us, has arranged for us to do her bidding by marshaling us with pain *and* pleasure. It's extremely important that we not feel so happy all the time that we don't get the work done or feel so sad all the time that we don't get the work done."

(The following is off point but amusing, and so I include it: reading further in Lykken's article "The Heritability of Happiness" in the *Harvard Mental Health Letter,* I was diverted by— and have no memory as to the pertinence of—an absolutely charming and unintentionally hilarious paragraph about homosexuals, starting with a mention of his wife's cousin, a man who "brought joy and new life into any room he entered. He was funny . . . a delightful and imaginative host, an ideal guest . . ." He goes on to mention that these qualities were wonderfully embodied by William Hurt in *Kiss of the Spider Woman* as well as Harvey Fierstein. "Only the intractably homophobic would fail to get a lift when he enters the room. What I am suggesting is that gay men, at least those with more feminine natures, seem to make an art of daily living, they enliven the tedious, decorate the drab, make the mundane more amusing . . . Perhaps the euphemism 'gay' is more apt than I had previously thought."

Clearly Dr. Lykken has neither had his path blocked by twenty feet of retractable dog leash unreeled across the sidewalk, just so that some narcissistic, over-muscled invert's pug—imaginatively named Will or Grace or *Liza*—might walk unimpeded by tax-paying humans, nor, I'm guessing, has Dr. Lykken been the opposite of helped by one of the evil queens on staff at Barneys, but on behalf of my fellow deviants, I would like to say—as I sit here in my own sodomitically bedizened surroundings [*the silks, the brocades, the stuffed cockatoo in the golden cage!*]—thank you, sir.)

I wasn't getting any work done. At T minus nine days, I startled out of sleep an hour before the alarm, at 5:00 AM, hissing, "Who the *hell* do you think you are?"—the words out of my mouth before I was fully conscious. I often resort to precisely this little pep talk to myself to get it together and stop fucking around— a cautionary admonition against sloth, usually uttered when I feel I've either eaten too much or am lying in bed too long. I sat down and began transcribing my notes. Some time before 9:00, I picked up the phone to call Martin Seligman himself. He had been very nice when setting up the interview, which made me feel like a shitheel. I tried to clear my mind of prejudicial thoughts, reminding myself who was the learned professional with numerous advanced degrees and who was the smart-ass faux journalist.

The phone was out. Mother*fucker.* I put on my sneakers and walked out to the corner to the pay phone to call repair. It was street-wide as there were already three people waiting on line. My mood briefly brightened to see that one of them was my next-door neighbor, a handsome Frenchman with a comically perfect V-shaped torso. As I crossed the street, one of the women pointed downtown and there, already in progress at the top of the horizon, a worst-case scenario even the most detail-obsessed defensive pessimist could not have foreseen. The first tower was on fire.

I never wrote the piece.

On the day I spent with Norem, both of us having no idea what would be transpiring mere weeks later, I had asked her if she thought it was all going to change, citing the Kruger and

Dunning study where optimists got a ticket back to earth when faced with the truth. Would the culture finally come up against reality and temper folks' rampant enthusiasm in the absence of facts, I wondered? "It had better change," she answered. "What's been celebrated in the media for the last ten years were all these twenty-two-year-old dot-com zillionaires, and they were all really optimistic and a lot of people were really optimistic about them in a pretty unnuanced and stupid way. And things have gone well for them, and they made money during the boom years and are perfectly willing to take credit for all their financial astuteness, even though you had to be an idiot if you didn't make money during those years, apparently. I didn't," she added.

Julie Norem is my kind of girl, I thought at that moment, not knowing that by "my kind of girl" I meant oblivious to the point of consigning Madonna to the dustbin of history. We were both so very wrong. Not wrong in the way everyone not privy to a daily intelligence briefing about bin Laden being determined to strike in the United States was wrong, but because we both grievously misread the tenacity of American glee and its extreme resistance to sharing the emotional spotlight with doubt. Rather than blasting open the doors to allow negative thinking into the public consciousness, the September 11 attacks only seemed to galvanize the optimists to new, adamantine heights of impenetrable positivity. Optimism didn't just not go away; it became belligerent, aggressive. There was now officially no room for valenced emotions.

As Norem pointed out, "arguing *for* negative thinking, under certain circumstances, is very different from arguing *against* positive thinking." But the line had been drawn. One could no longer point out that doubts, when voiced, can give dimension to reasoning, improve performance, or stave off disaster. Just like the fallacious separation of the Happy from the Sad, it was both a false division and an intrinsic judgment. Contingency thinking, and contingency thinkers, became saddled with such ancillary traits as being counterproductive, not team players, killjoys, Cassandras, or worse: people whose allegiances were seriously in question, appeasers. In reality, it was no more traitorous than a parent looking out for the best interests of his child. Say you came to me, for example, contemplating a preemptive invasion of a sovereign nation (an incursion predicated on cooked intelligence, misinformation, and outright lies, but never mind), and you tried to convince me that said incursion would spread the honeyed sunshine of democracy and freedom upon a formerly dark corner of the world and occasion from the inhabitants of that sovereign nation nothing but full-throated greetings to you and your troops as liberators and the heaping upon you of grateful garlands. I might say, "Well, that's terrific, and best of luck on your dubiously noble and messianic project." But if I in turn add, "Before you go, have you checked that you have enough soldiers, adequately outfitted with sufficient gear? We don't want them scavenging the Baghdad rubbish heaps for scrap metal to fashion hillbilly armor, now, do we?" If that's *all* I said, just that little bit of small-voiced advocacy for some contingency planning. If I never once asked after the authenticity of those aerial photographs presented to the U.N. by Colin Powell (merely acting according to the tenets of the loyal soldier he was. Truly, if he's so bound by the ancient codes of honor, so haunted by the ghosts of the thousands of lives he is partially responsible for snuffing out, then let's go all ancient Sparta on his loyal soldier ass. Let him fall upon his sword or offer up his tender throat to the blade. Isn't that what they did back then? All that wrestling with himself on the Sunday morning news shows, the repellent too-little-too-late ex post facto tortured regret, his conscience-ridden resignation . . . well, all I can say is Yiddishists everywhere should bow down before this apotheosis of chutzpah. But let me be clear about this: Bush and Co. didn't lie because they are optimists. They lied because they are liars. Okay, back to the matter at hand . . .), supposing I didn't mention any of that, nor even the complicit looking the other way as soldiers were sold shitty, inadequate, extortionate insurance policies. If *all* I said was, "Hey buddy, looks like you'll need more soldiers, if only to protect all those vases," it does not necessarily follow that my contingency thinking nullifies your positive agenda, or that my advancing some more detailed cognition means that I lack patriotism.

See how that works?

Except that it almost never works. It is an almost unwinnable battle. American self-assurance and individuality lionize the can-do positivity of the optimist. It's what settled the prairies and built the railroads, I suppose, although I like to think it was the pessimists who had the anxious foresight to circle the wagons. Given the greater comforts of our lives off the frontier today, optimism seems even more like the natural choice. (It's presumptuous of me to assess your level of luxury, I know, but if you're reading this, chances are you're bobbing along in the same lavishly appointed boat as I am: an inhabitant of the developed world, at least, which in and of itself makes us very lucky indeed, and which makes those among us who *still* report feelings of dissatisfaction and anxiety seem very ungrateful.) That very privilege imbues all of us with a sense of power over cause and effect, a feeling that our actions can and do affect outcomes—which they sometimes do—but it remains among the prettiest of delusions, one that is ground down and out of most people elsewhere on this earth.

A 1999 article from *The New York Times* told the story of

the villagers of the Cambodian hamlet of Bet Trang. Coming upon three thousand tons of cement-like material in a nearby field, they could not believe their good fortune. The white plastic of the sacks proved to have manifold uses, as ground sheets, tents, waterproofing, emptied out for grain storage, you name it. What a boon, until, of course the villagers developed headaches, diarrhea, and weight loss. Eventually it was found that the powder, compressed ash from an industrial incinerator, contained insane amounts of mercury and other hazardous metals. It was dumped there by the Formosa Plastics Corporation of Taiwan. And why was the waste dumped in Cambodia and not the country formerly known as Formosa? Because the comparatively wealthy citizenry of Taiwan had a first-world sense of liberty and entitlement, and an opinion about the poisoning of their habitat, and they understandably protested. But the Cambodian villagers did not complain, even as they got sicker and sicker. This calamity seemed not materially different from everything else they had endured over centuries of colonization and fratricidal civil war. They had been taught to expect nothing from this life. Certainly nothing good.

Buddhist detachment might have it all over Western notions of jealousy, guilt, covetousness, and general engagement in its deep understanding of the essentially amoral random anarchy of the universe. Asian cultures score more pessimistically on diagnostic measures, tending to value the self-effacing aspects of self-doubt. With less value placed upon positive emotion, there is less impetus for gratuitous optimism. But just like those anxious, sad-sack Westerners, there are, of course, exceptions everywhere. My friend Jim went to see Amma, the Indian mystic whose hugs, it is said, are a dose of extra-strength sympathy and benevolence (she dispenses these hugs to audiences around the world, including America, so her fans must be Western in some healthy percentage). Amma is said to be a conduit of all the love of the universe channeled through one pair of arms, a single warm body plugging into the great celestial wellspring of lovingkindness. Jim, a man of perhaps the sweetest disposition I have ever known and an avowed optimist—he wrote a beautiful chapbook of poems devoted to it—waited for something like four hours in Madison Square Garden and was incredibly glad he did.

The best I can manage is a tepid, "If you say so." I love a hug as much as the next guy, but I need a context of familiarity, some reason to believe that said hug is meant for me specifically. Being touched can be lovely, transcendent even, but a hug is almost deeper than eye contact, as meaningful as a kiss. A hug that one waits in line for from a woman who wouldn't know me if I stood up in her soup would be like reading a piece of direct mail and being warmed by its repeated use of my name ("and if you act now, *DAVID RAKOFF*, we'll also send you . . ."). I would feel duped and even lonelier than before, like stuffing the other side of the bed with clothes and making like it's a boyfriend.

The embrace of another clearly has some salubrious effect. Babies definitely need them, we all do. But a hug bestowed so freely to a stadium full of people, without prejudice or favor—while lovely and humbling in its benevolence—might also be seen by someone who cannot help but transfuse everything with his negativity as debauching the very nature of what it means to connect with another person, which requires hours and hours, not of waiting in line but of putting in the time getting to know someone. That harboring of initial illusions and hopes, the eventual downgrading of same, the word-filled, prone-to-recrimination-and-betrayal nuisance of it all, and the *still* continuing to rely upon, be relied upon in turn, be dismayed by, argue with, and withal love another human being. It's the difference between sugar and complex carbohydrates. It might be more fun to eat in the short run, but it's markedly less sustaining in the long.

But to tap still more deeply into the churlish vein, it is the belief in the extra-soothing power of the universe that gets me since, as best as I can determine, the universe cares not one jot for you or me. It really doesn't. As the writer Melissa Bank points out, the only proper response to a tearful "Why me?" is, sadly, "Why *not* you?" The sunniest, most positive child in Malaysia laboring in a fucking sneaker factory can visualize all the good fortune he wants, but without concrete changes in international models of global trade, finance, and educational opportunities along with some very temporal man-made policies, just for starters, guess where he's going tomorrow morning? (A hint: it rhymes with *schmucking sneaker factory.*)

That can be a cold and lonely reality with which to contend, and one to which every one of us, even the most vinegar-soaked pessimist, is naturally resistant. We all spend our lives rejecting this truth and, consciously or not, entreating the universe—with its vast stretches of deep space, dark matter, and uncharted, immeasurable distances—to somehow align itself in sheer admiration of our fervor and gumption, to rain down precisely that which it is we wish for.

And the universe will say nothing.

Even the most charmed life is a veritable travelogue of disappointment. There will always be an inevitable gulf between hope and reality. It is how we traverse these Deserts of Letdown that shows us what we are made of (perhaps almost as much as does choosing to characterize them as Deserts of Letdown).

"Such sand this is!" some of us will moan, fretting our way

along, grain by melancholy grain. (Is that a Yiddish inflection you hear? I leave you to draw your own conclusions.) "Sand?" others will answer, briefly bewildered and barreling across, unmindful of their burning feet.

But look: There we all are (and in the following everyone seems to be in agreement); moving forward, like it or not.

Shrimp

Nothing assails the writer's credibility more than the pleasant childhood. I freely admit to having had one myself. A happy fact reflected sadly in my book sales. And yet I'd sooner do most anything short of putting needles in my eyes than willingly remember what it was like to have been a child. Things were not terrible. I was neither beaten nor abused. No dank cellars or chilly garrets for me. Neither my trust nor my body were violated by a clergyman or a beloved family friend. I was safe and sound.

No, indeed, I freely admit to having had all the accoutrements that make for a lovely childhood, one replete with the perquisites of great creature comfort, in a bustling and cultured metropolis, in a home decorated in typical late-twentieth-century secular-humanist Jewish psychiatrist: African masks, paintings both abstract and figurative, framed museum posters, Marimekko bedspreads. And listen, on the hi-fi, why it's *The Weavers at Carnegie Hall* or *Jacques Brel Is Alive and Well and Living in Paris*. Or is that Miriam Makeba, clicking her way through a Xhosa lullaby? And on the bookshelf, among the art monographs, the Saul Bellow and Philip Roth novels, the Günter Grass first editions, collected *New Yorkers*, Time-Life Great Books, *National Geographics*, and *Horizon* magazines, there tucked in behind the

Encyclopedia Judaica, you might just find that old illustrated copy of *The Joy of Oral Sex,* a gag gift never thrown out.

Mealtimes were filled with sprightly talk, with each member of the family given their conversational due. Weekends involved regular outings to museums to look at Henry Moore sculptures, or dinosaur bones, then off to the gift shop to buy a liver-speckled cowrie shell or dried sea horse for one thin dime. There were trips to the theater and the ballet, annually to New York City to see relatives and Broadway shows, and to buy an amethyst geode at the gem store on Thirty-fourth and Madison, and excursions even farther afield, to Spain or London or back to the old country where we, the children of the New World, could be shown off to the relations left behind. Yes, I can say with no fear of contradiction that, as the indulged youngest of three, mine was a golden upbringing, under the loving guidance and tutelage of two caring and adoring parents whose own path was illuminated by the sunlight they were convinced shone straight out of my ass.

And still, I loathed being a child. Plainly stated, being a child was not—as used to be said around the time that I *was* a child— my bag. Childhood was a foreign country to me. Everyone has an internal age. A time in life when one is, if not one's best, then at the very least one's most authentic self. When your outside and inside are in sync, and soma and psyche mesh as perfectly as they're ever going to. I always felt that my internal clock was calibrated somewhere between forty-seven and fifty-three years old. I don't want to make it seem like I was so smart or mature or advanced. I did all right for myself, but I was off the charts in only one respect, remarkably so. I was tiny. I come from a short family, but I was worryingly diminutive. Freakishly small. I knew some others who were below average in size, but they usually made up for it by being athletic or . . . straight. I was not one of the shouting, jostling, hockey-loving boys, and I also wasn't a girl. I was what used to be called a Big Fag.

In E. B. White's 1945 classic, *Stuart Little,* the protagonist is the second son of Mrs. Frederick C. Little of New York City. A child who was "not much bigger than a mouse" and who also "looked very much like a mouse in every way." Stuart was articulate beyond his years. Stuart had a flair for costume, dressing up in the full regalia of vaguely pornographic sailor whites just to visit the Boat Pond in Central Park. When my second-grade teacher, Mrs. Brailey—perhaps the only woman I have ever truly loved—read *Stuart Little* to us, I remember thinking *Yes!* This confluence of traits: the unquestioned membership in a family despite one glaring material difference from them all, the tininess only seeming to accentuate the courtly manners and dandy tendencies . . . this was me. I *was* Stuart Little.

Or so I fervently wished. I lacked Stuart Little's self-possession. His ease in the world. Stuart Little was only afraid of dogs, whereas I was polymorphously phobic, scared of everything: dogs, heights, subways, crowds, snakes, the dark, elevators, tunnels, bridges, spiders, flying, loud noises, roller coasters, amusement-park midways, the ruffians who hung around same, horror movies, fireworks, rock music that seemed to glorify chemical abandon, balloons blown up too big, changing lightbulbs, athletes, going down into the basement . . . everything was freighted with terror.

I vibrated with anxiety. Tight as a watch spring, skittish as a chihuahua, when I wasn't bursting into tears, I covered my overarching trepidation with a loud-mouthed bravura. I was highly unpleasant. I'm not fishing here. It dawned on me recently that even though I have published books and lived through a bout of cancer, barely a handful of people from my childhood have ever attempted to contact me, and I don't blame them one bit.

Stuart Little, having set out for the open road to seek his fortune, finds himself the substitute teacher in a one-room schoolhouse, a position he manages to secure simply by donning the professorial drag of striped trousers, tweed jacket with waistcoat, and a pince-nez. The children are rapt by his cunning size and stern air of authority. In a lesson on ethics, he has one of the boys steal a small sachet from one of the girls. Stuart turns his attention to the purloined pillow, which attracts him; it might make a lovely, fragrant bed:

"That's a very pretty thing," said Stuart, trying to hide his eagerness. "You don't want to sell it, do you?"

"Oh, no," replied Katherine. "It was a present to me."

"I suppose it was given you by some boy you met at Lake Hopatcong last summer and it reminds you of him," he says to her, dreamily.

"Yes, it was," said Katherine, blushing.

"Ah," said Stuart, "summers are wonderful, aren't they, Katherine?"

Stuart Little, at this point in the story, is seven years old. And yet here he is, transformed into Thomas Mann's Aschenbach. The aging roué, his summers of love and beauty all far behind him, now watching the erotic play of the youngsters on the Venice Lido as the plague creeps in.

How I wished that I, too, might be able to skip directly to adulthood in just the same way. Not so much so that I would be big but so that I might be done with all this and enjoy some peace. Grown-ups, it seemed to me, didn't have to play sports. Grown-ups didn't have farting contests (this was decades before Johnny Knoxville and his anal-obsessive *Jackass* pranksters). Grown-ups, in general, seemed more indulgent of others' problems, each having so many of their own. If I could make it to adulthood, I would be able to join their tolerant ranks and no one would mind my size.

Until such time, I could usually divert people's attention away from my physical lack by trotting out an advanced vocabulary, or displaying some sort of comic timing, or making a Yukio Mishima reference. And then, like the trout tickler who has cooled his hand in the stream for long enough that the fish doesn't even feel itself being picked up out of the water, there would come a moment where I knew I had my listener. There would be a subtle change in their faces, an inclining forward. Their features would assemble themselves, focused upon me in an attitude of almost perplexed amusement.

There is a reason it is called charm. It is a trick, and like all false magic, it never lasts. Eventually even the most gullible rube will begin to examine the rising table, or ferret out the source of the one-for-yes, two-for-no knocking from the spirit world. And then he sees the sham. Just as quickly as people's faces went a little bit dreamy, I could see them blink themselves back to reality. *I'm talking to a child,* they would suddenly realize. Like in a cartoon, where the concussion's halo of revolving stars is dissipated by a vigorous shake of the head, they would look at me with a kind of *what was I thinking* self-reproach. I had been caught out, once again.

At age fourteen, I remember being at a family party, talking to a woman I did not know. She taught classics at a high school in Toronto, as I recall. We were having a nice conversation until the moment when I mentioned, yet again, something about ninth grade—or, as we called it in Canada, grade nine. She made an exaggerated gulp, bugged her eyes out a little, and crossing her surprised hands upon her collarbone, said, "I'm sorry, did you say *grade* nine?"

"Yes," I replied, knowing exactly where this was leading.

"Oh my," she said, smiling. "All this time I thought you were telling me you *were* nine." She playfully pushed me on the shoulder in an *Oh, you* gesture, like this was some stunt I had put over on her, which I suppose it was. She smiled companionably. My size was a joke we could share in equally. *I thought that was a hideous, horrible mask you were wearing but it's actually your face! Aren't you clever and funny!*

I was four foot nine when I entered tenth grade. The local public high school was an institution catering primarily to teen Jewish royalty, as my brother called us. I could not compete in the arms race of wardrobe and accessories, and I didn't try. Happily, my size also meant that I didn't have to even feign interest in the erotic play between the boys and the girls. One look at me was all you needed to know that that would be writing checks my ass couldn't cover.

Like generations of other misfits before me, be they morphological, sexual, or otherwise, I decided that I would make theater my refuge. I was a pretty good actor as a child, albeit with the budding homosexual's propensity for *schmacting,* the overuse of outsized and non-contextual emotion. I could cry on cue and did so whenever I got the chance, which was mainly alone in my bedroom in front of the mirror—great heaving arias of melodramatic hysteria that could burst forth with all the vulgar hoopla of a magician's bouquet.

The nonmusical offering each year was directed by the drama teacher herself. She selected ambitious works like Brecht's harrowing *Mother Courage and Her Children,* which made liberal use of burlap and brown makeup smudged onto cheeks to evoke the filth and hardship of the Thirty Years' War. Another time it was *David and Lisa,* which was about two adolescent mental patients. David was hyperintellectual and didn't like to be touched, while Lisa was a bubbling free spirit, given to rhyming echolalia. This was one of those plays from the 1960s that equated insanity with deep artistic sensitivity, asking the disingenuous question, *Who is to say who is crazy? You? I? Perhaps it is the mad who are truly sane!* It was considered bad form at the time to posit that the muttering fellow in the corner scratching Bible verses into his forearm with a fork seemed a little bit, I don't know, off?

That year's offering was to be *The Ecstasy of Rita Joe,* a work that dealt with the social problems and injustices facing Canada's native population. It was the 1970s, so we were still calling them Indians. A gritty drama, *Rita Joe* was unrelieved by even the faintest glimmer of levity or hope, ending with a spectacularly brutal gang rape and murder of its woebegone heroine. Precisely the kind of deeply earnest downer that only a bunch of teenagers would dare put on.

I could not wait.

The drama classroom was in a portable, one-room prefabricated building on cinder blocks in the middle of the schoolyard. It was a shoes-off environment, no desks, just wall-to-wall nylon broadloom in a mottled goldenrod. The carpet was pilled, matted with staples and crumbs, and waxy with years of adolescent foot sweat. About fifteen hopefuls sat on the floor in a circle around the drama teacher, who sat with her legs folded under her, Zen tea master–like. She surveyed us and then her eyes lit upon me. She gave me a small smile, the corners of her mouth turning up slightly, while at the same time from her nose I could hear a small puff, the softest whisper of breath. The sound a pillow makes when you sink your head into it. The exhalation pushed her head back and up in the opposite direction ever so slightly.

"I'm sorry," she said to me, before she even handed out the saffron-yellow script books. "I'm afraid I can't even let you audition. I'm going to need actors who are more physically substantial."

There are some moments in life that are perfect. Not necessarily wonderful, but that hew so closely to some Platonic or ruminated-upon version of themselves that one almost can't believe they are happening. In fact, one doesn't believe they are happening. As a freshman in college, for example, walking along 112th Street of a winter's evening, the Cathedral of Saint John the Divine just up ahead, I looked over to my left at the garbage bags in the empty lot at the corner. In the fading purple gloaming, their surfaces swirled, they seemed to be undulating. I remember thinking to myself, *What an amazing trick of the light, because it is almost as if those garbage bags were simply covered with live rats, but of course, they're not, because to see that with my own eyes would be too horrible, too scarring, too much exactly what I fear at this moment on this dark New York side street. Ergo, here be no rats.*

On I marched right up to those selfsame Hefty bags which, of course, were covered, *teeming* with starving rats who squeaked en masse, a horrible, squealing rodent choir, that scattered upon my approach, some of them almost running over my boots.

So when the drama teacher said, "I'm going to need actors who are more physically substantial," essentially announcing to the room "this production is only open to people with pubic hair, which you emphatically do not yet seem to have," they were so exactly the words of which I lived in fear, the words I anticipated coming out of everyone's mouth, that I didn't get it at first. I thought I was still making it up in my head. She was smiling at me, after all, and I smiled back the entire time, Wile E. Coyote blithely walking off his butte into thin air and not falling until he actually realizes there is nothing beneath his feet but ether. I once heard about an Austro-Hungarian princess, assassinated by an anarchist who, pretending to bump into her, actually stabbed her through the heart with a long pin. Nobody even knew she had been mortally wounded, least of all she herself, until hours later when she finally collapsed. She lived a life as rarefied and abstemious as a silkworm, subsisting on a ridiculous diet (mulberry leaves and shaved ice in a silver bowl comes to mind, but I think I'm making that up, since it sounds suspiciously like what one actually feeds silkworms). Daily, Her Highness forced herself into heavily corseted black garments. So constricted was she, so inky the fabric, that she didn't register the pin breaching her chest wall, nor did anyone else notice that her blood-soaked dress was darker and heavier than usual. In fact, until she dropped dead, she apparently just smiled and smiled.

As did I. Still grinning and hot-faced, I got to my feet and left the circle. I walked to the door and found my shoes among the pile of sneakers. I laced them up. I found my jacket and my knapsack. The drama teacher had moved on at this point and was already asking other students to read from the play as I stepped outside and closed the door behind me.

Years later, in college, I was working as a summer researcher in a psychiatric hospital when one of the younger patients on the floor—a boy exactly my age who had been sent home from school after a schizophrenic episode—showed up at my office door. Formal patient contact wasn't part of my job, but I wasn't forbidden from talking to them, either. I had been instructed to treat them all with respect and kindness, but this boy freaked me out. The differences between us seemed insufficiently pronounced, without even a discernible before-and-after split screen to separate us. It felt like I, too, might go crazy at any moment, just from being in close enough contact with him. Secondhand psychosis.

He was agitated and holding his notebook in one hand, which he held out to me, open to a page.

"Look at this," he said.

Exhaustive tables of German verb conjugations covered the paper, written in the tiny, meticulous hand that seems to be the sole province of the mentally troubled.

"Those look like German verbs," I said.

"Yes, I know what they are," he said, nodding his head impatiently. "What I want to know is who wrote them."

Without even thinking about it, I gave him a smile accompanied by a small nasal puff of air whose gentle shotgun report pushed my head back in an upward nod.

Here's where things get weird in an almost *Bleak House* coincidence. I saw my high-school drama teacher that very same summer, on the street right outside that very same psychiatric hospital (she could have been on her way to Chinatown for dim sum, I suppose, but c'mon . . .). As the child of a shrink, I knew enough to respect her privacy. I would let her initiate the contact if she wanted it. But I wanted to convey to her that I finally understood that smile. It was a smile meant to sweeten a gentle admonition, a friendly entreaty, as if to plead, *Please don't make me complicit in your delusion.* A smile that says, *Can't you see it? You have eyes. Look at yourself.*

I watched her as she furtively shifted her eyes away from mine quickly, so as to pretend she hadn't seen me at all. I didn't blame her for not wanting to stop and talk, and I didn't really mind. She was probably having a hard day. Besides, by that time I had grown.

Isn't It Romantic?

The paper is crisp from the wheat paste used to put it up on a wall just off West Houston Street in 1988 or thereabouts. It was still damp when I carefully peeled it from the bricks. It graced a bathroom door in a former apartment but now stays rolled up among the various posters for which I have neither wall space nor funds to frame. A text-only broadside, its forceful font (center aligned, all caps, sans serif) is as no-nonsense as its in-your-face message: MURDER DAN QUAYLE IN COLD BLOOD, it reads (remember when we thought Dan Quayle the very apex of incompetence and the absolute nadir of elected officialdom?). Along with a cherished READ MY LIPS ACT UP T-shirt and a largely intact strip of SUPPORT VAGINAL PRIDE stickers from WHAM! (Women's Health Action and Mobilization), it is a reminder of how much of a battleground the city was at that time, during the early-ish days of the pandemic; some desperately-needed humor in response to those very unfunny circumstances. If the occasional joke crossed the line of good taste, so be it. Shocking the status quo has always been the job of art. Art was salvation, art was revolution. There was a war going on and the soldiers were those engaged in the deadly serious and downright heroic business of making art.

Just look at them: young, multiracial, and beautifully ragtag in thrift-store clothing (disregard for the moment those anachronistic headsets), singing with an earnest fervor and committed self-regard that the Bolsheviks storming the Winter Palace would have had a hard time mustering. And what are they telling us? That there are 525,600 minutes in a year.

Wait, what? That's the grand statement? The kind of pointless breakdown that calls to mind that damp-nosed, pedantic boy in school who was always volunteering useless information, like how much Belgium weighs. But here, in the musical *Rent,* the updating of Puccini's *La Bohème* to New York City in those desperate days, this is anything but dry fact. It is an exhortation to each and every one of us to mindfully mark the passing of these 525,600 minutes. Do not dole them out into the despairing mounds of Prufrock's coffee spoons, but rather celebrate them in something Jonathan Larson, the composer and lyricist, called "Seasons of Love."

What does that even mean, Seasons of Love? The mind might conjure a soft-core calendar. There is Miss April, coyly covering an areola with a gerbera daisy, while Miss December shields her nipples behind fluffy angora-mitten-clad hands (*toasty!*). Or perhaps Seasons of Love® would be something you'd keep in the door of the fridge. Seasons of Love® might come in a foil-wrapped cardboard can with a shaker top. Dehydrated onion would figure prominently. As would carnauba wax. Eventually it would be taken off the market when it came to light that the bacon bits were nothing more than highly salted, air-puffed balsa wood, but before all that there would be television commercials showing happy couples sprinkling their Seasons of Love® over salads, or laughingly feeding one another bites of baked potato festively speckled with the stuff, like someone had just celebrated New Year's all over your food.

In *Rent,* the characters live out their Seasons of Love in huge

Manhattan lofts. Some of them have AIDS, which, coincidentally, is also the name of a dreaded global pandemic that is still raging and has killed millions of people worldwide. In *Rent*, AIDS seems only to render one cuter and cuter. The characters are artists. Creative types. Some of them are homosexual, and the ones who aren't don't seem to mind. They screen their calls and when it is their parents they roll their eyes. They hate their parents. They are never going back to Larchmont, no way. They will stay here, living in their two thousand square feet of picturesque poverty, being sexually free and creative.

And who can blame them? It can be delightful and interesting to spend one's days engaged in carnal hijinks and creative pursuits. Exponentially more delightful and interesting than a life of responsibility-shouldering, paper-pushing drudgery. Fraught and messy though an artistic life may be, is there a drug that can induce the euphoria as energizing as that intensely fragile moment when the muse passes through one and the artist becomes the simultaneously perfect and flawed instrument of expression? No, there is not. Even as the inner voices battle it out, intoning "You suck!" and "Eureka!" in equal measure, creation is—like the loosest of teeth just begging to be toggled by the curious tongue—a joyous torment, in whatever form it takes.

Some examples:
- A composer plinks out a tune on a piano. His raking hands—raw, overlarge paddles at the ends of his bony wrists—have turned his hair into a mad dandelion. His shirt collar is frayed. A lack of nourishment, either because he cannot afford to eat or he is too immersed in his work to even *think* about food, has given him the gaunt ethereality of an El Greco saint. The garret

radiator clanks and hisses. He scratches a few notes on some music paper. He plinks some more. Suddenly he crashes both hands down on the keyboard, then bringing them quickly up to his head, he grabs the hair at his temples in angry fistfuls and screams, "It. Won't. Work!" (Alternately, in a fit of brilliant madness, he transcribes onto music paper the pattern of the birds sitting on the telephone wires outside his window and thereby finishes his masterwork, *Requiem for the Common Pigeon*.)

- Beside a clanking and hissing garret radiator, a novelist sits at a typewriter, beside him a shot glass with the amber dregs of his morning Bushmills. He is reading the page he's just written. Realizing that it's shit, he tears it from the platen and tosses it behind him. Cut to the wastebasket overflowing with crumpled paper.

- Four AM, a wife rolls over in bed, her arm touching the absence on the other side of the mattress. Rising, she ties her thin flannel wrapper around her (the garret radiator, usually clanking and hissing, is now cold and silent due to unpaid utility bills), and makes her way down the hall, pushing open the door of the studio. Silently she watches the hulking, ropy back of her husband as he stands before his unfinished canvas. Her eyes fill with tears of love and she turns to go back to bed, forgetting for the moment the yellow-purple sunset on her left cheek, the cost—a cost she is happy to pay—of having married a genius. (Let us pause herewith for a moment of honesty about that old chestnut about art and artists being immune to the petty concerns of morality, or the need to be kind, or fair, or in fact anything other than obliteratingly self-involved. It has always seemed little more than a rationalization for goatish, flesh-pressing painters, writers, and musicians to skip out on checks, borrow but not return things, sire but not take care of children, and mostly to cheat on, mooch off of, or sock long-suffering wives and girlfriends.)

- Consider, even, that well-worn cliché, not of an artist, exactly, but certainly an easily bruised sensitivity and a deep well of pain, speaking to a definite creative bent: the Sad and Beautiful French Girl with the Enviable Pair of Tits Who Is Slowly Going Mad. How do we know that she is slowly going mad? There she is (top-less, natch), looking at her reflection in the mirror as if gazing at a stranger. Watch as she puts on her lipstick, gradually smearing ever-wider circles outside the edges of her mouth while fat, photogenic glycerin tears fall silently down her perfect cheeks.

Here is what the characters do in *Rent* to show us that they are creative: nothing. They do nothing. The "songwriter" spends fourteen seconds noodling on his guitar, sampling Puccini. The "filmmaker" shoots a lot of Super 8 footage of people he knows, which makes him about as much of an artist as every-body's dad. Nobody is pasting up a poster or mimeographing a pamphlet. Vice President Quayle suits them just fine. A few of the dramatis personae have jobs, but this only makes them laughably contemptible corporate stooges. There is one charac-ter who actually works at her art, a newly-minted lesbian per-formance artist named Maureen whose ambition is portrayed as being as unseemly, rapacious, and untrustworthy as her elastic Kinsey placement. All of it evidence of a callous narcissism (*"She needs someone to run the light board? Fucking bitch . . .*"). Right up there alongside the retrovirus and the forces of gentrification, Maureen is the villain of the piece. She should stop with these constant careerist attempts at being "interesting." In addition to being unattractive, they're unnecessary. An artist is something you are, not something you do.

I first encountered this Seussian syllogism in a used-book store, where I spent an extra thirty minutes fake-browsing just so I might continue to eavesdrop on the cashier, who was expounding to his friend about *Johnny Got His Gun*, Dalton Trumbo's classic antiwar novel. The cashier had a theory about the book's protagonist, Johnny, wounded and blinded and amputated to such an extent that, while sentient, he was little more than an unresponsive trunk of meat with a rich inner life. "So I asked myself: If this guy was Picasso, would he have been any less of an artist or less of a genius just because he couldn't paint? And my thinking is no, he wouldn't." I lacked the bravery to challenge him more openly than a muttered "Oh, brother" from the stacks, choosing instead to ridicule and sell him out years later, here in print. But it's the same reasoning: indolence as proof positive of prodigious gifts. You can arguably invent Cubism and be the very embodiment of Modernism if you get a kick out of that sort of thing. But you hardly *need* to, Armless Picasso. Artists are artists whether they produce or not. None of it requires much more than hanging out.

And hanging out can be marvelous. But hanging out does not make one an artist. A secondhand wardrobe does not make one an artist. Neither do a hair-trigger temper, melancholic nature, propensity for tears, hating your parents, nor even HIV—I hate to say it—none of these make one an artist. They can help, but just as being gay does not make one witty (you can suck a mile of cock, as my friend Sarah Thyre puts it, it still won't make you

Oscar Wilde, believe me), the only thing that makes one an artist is making art. And that requires the precise opposite of hanging out; a deeply lonely and unglamorous task of tolerating oneself long enough to push something out.

So when they sing in the anthem of the show (a lie, really. Every song in the show is an anthem, delivered with adolescent earnestness. It's like being trapped in the humid pages of a teenager's diary), when they sing in the *title* anthem of the show, "*We're not gonna pay this year's rent,*" followed by a kind of barked cheer of "*rent rent rent rent rent!,*" my only question is: Well, *why* aren't you going to pay this year's rent?

It seems that they're not going to pay this year's rent because rent is for losers and uncreative types. Rent is for Suits, while they are the last bastion of artistic purity. They have not sold out and yet their brilliance goes unacknowledged, *so fuck you, yuppie scum!*

Jonathan Larson died the day before *Rent* opened. He went home from the dress rehearsal feeling poorly, made himself a pot of tea, and died on his kitchen floor. It is an achingly sad story; a waste of a huge talent and, by all accounts, a truly lovely guy. It is made all the more theatrically wrenching by the fact that the show went on to become a huge Pulitzer-garnering hit; the aging Calvero, Charlie Chaplin's character in *Limelight,* expiring in the wings as Claire Bloom's ballerina triumphs. I heard 9/11 jokes long before it felt okay to say that even though it was a terrible thing that he died and that, yes, AIDS is a devastating, horrible scourge to which I have lost many friends, and indeed New York was becoming far too expensive and criminally inhospitable to young people who tried to come here with dreams of making art, and how regrettable that the town's vibrancy and authenticity were being replaced by a culture-free, high-end-retail cluster-fuck of luxury condo buildings whose all-glass walls essentially require a populace that doesn't own bookshelves or, consequently, books. A metropolis of streets once thriving with local businesses and services now consisting of nothing but Marc Jacobs store after Marc Jacobs store and cupcake purveyors (is there anything more blandly sweet, less evocative of this great city, and more *goyish* than any other baked good with the possible exception of Eucharist wafers than the cupcake?). And even though Jonathan Larson's musical was meant in its own ham-fisted, undergraduate way to be a call to arms against this very turn of events, was it just me, or was this middlebrow lie a symptom posing as an antidote, like watching a sex-ed film narrated by gonorrhea? Were others also leaving the theater rooting for the landlords?

Larson worked for years at a diner right around the corner from an apartment I once had. Restaurant work can be punishing and thankless toil, so he is to be applauded for plying his craft so steadfastly after what must have been long shifts on his feet. His is the story of almost every artist. Why, then, in transmuting his own struggle did he so completely drop the ball? (And to those of you who say that dumbing down and sugaring up is innate to musical theater, I say fuck you, homophobe. Go listen to the dark brilliance of *Pal Joey* or *Floyd Collins* and then come and talk to me.) Perhaps it is an added sense of identification that fuels my sense of betrayal. In photographs of Larson, with his heavy features and hooded eyes—the sweet and approachable face wishing like hell it could make the leap to handsome— I see my own.

And yet part of me understands fully. I'm an idiot but I'm not stupid. I get it that representation is reality's more photogenic flip side. It's best not to think too closely on what Elizabeth's and Darcy's teeth must have actually been like. Or those windswept heroes in countless Romantic paintings, standing on their solitary crags, gazing out Byronically over the roiling sea. It's all beautiful desolation and man-against-the-elements-emergence-of-the-Self-birth-of-the-Modern fabulous; for the first time in history, masters of their own fates, their minds steeled and alert in the bracing sea air. The canvas gives no hint, nor should it, of the challenging trek it must have taken to reach those wave-washed spits of land, nor the malodorous discomfort of those sodden, pre-Gore-Tex garments, the chafing cotton and the lead-heavy wool. And underneath all that soaked and salty clothing, the poet's skin, an angry red canvas of papulae and chilblains.

The Myth of the Bohemian persists with good reason. Given the choice between a day spent giving oneself over to oil painting, or one spent in the confining grid of office cubicles, most folks would opt for the old fantasy of the carnal chaos of drop cloths, easels, turpentine, raffia-wrapped Chianti bottles holding drippy candle ends, and cavorting nude models, forgetting momentarily the lack of financial security and the necessary hours and hours of solitude spent fucking up over and over again.

I lived in Brooklyn a long time ago, with my best friend, Natalia, on the second floor of a small two-story coach house. The basement still had its red dirt floor from the nineteenth century. We were a block away from a jail, in the heart of the borough's Penal District (not yet a real estate term, but just wait). Across from the stately courthouse was a beautiful stretch of century-old brownstones, a sagging and wearily voluptuous rock pile, every straight line worn down over the years to a gentle curve. The windows had ancient, flaking gold-foil letters for the offices of bail bondsmen and ambulance-chasing lawyers. On the uninterrupted brick face of the westernmost side, an old wall advertisement touting DIVORCES: $99! in an oddly cheerful font. During the day, the streets hummed with activity; a photogenic, Runyonesque bustle of lawyers, judges, perps, and private dicks, but at night, it was an absolute dead zone.

My neighbors directly across the street were a family of pit-bull-owning drug dealers. Their fort was held down by a mother and her young son, Seymour, and adolescent daughter, Vickie, along with an intermittent cast of male characters. It was during these years and from this family that I learned, intimately, the words *maricón* and *pendejo*. Two doors down from them, a neon sign in a window advertised DELICES DE SAIGON, although in the four years that I lived there, I saw no signs of life from that building, delicious, Vietnamese, or otherwise. Directly beside us lived a reclusive Bakelite-radio enthusiast whose apartment was a hangout for a gaggle of boys from the nearby homeless shelter. We could hear him screaming at them ceaselessly through the bathroom wall.

Once you got indoors, the apartment was essentially perfect. A lovely and cheerful place with folding wooden shutters, and a working fireplace clad in green slate to augment the feeble efforts of the old gas heater in the winter. In the summer, the windows on both sides were a fine substitute for air-conditioning. For the occasional heat wave—those stretches when the cool-down strategy of switching to menthols simply didn't work, when one moved about the city irritable, aphasic with sleeplessness, and salty as a deer lick—there was a box fan, purchased at the nearby Abraham and Straus department store. I had been surprised to find that the thing actually came with directions, beyond "plug in and turn on." The best way to cool a room, according to the ancient, pretech principles of cross-ventilation, is to place a fan facing out the window farthest away from you. This will force the warm air from the apartment, while drawing air from the outside through the windows nearer by. I did it. It worked. I switched back to regular cigarettes.

Standing at the kitchen sink, we could look out the window at the huge plane and flowering chestnut trees in the surprisingly lush backyards of the whole block. And no plot was wilder or greener than the one directly beneath the kitchen window, an overgrown jungle at the back of an old single-room-occupancy* rooming house. The house was as untamed as its garden. It appeared that the entire cubic volume of every room was filled with stuff, Collyer brothers–style: ironing boards, cardboard suitcases, electric toasters and fans, plastic bags cinched and bulging, laundry baskets swelling like wine barrels, all of it piled up, floor to ceiling, right to the windows. The most visible resident was an old alcoholic woman, not a day under seventy. Natalia and I had dubbed her "Madame Balzac" for some reason. (Why exactly has been erased by the years. I've only ever read one Balzac novel, but we were in our smart-ass twenties. I think it had something to do with our Madame's habit of lobbing her garbage out of her windows into the yard. Perhaps a character did something similar in *Père Goriot?* Who can remember . . .) When not seated on the front stoop in a soiled, threadbare black

---

*Single Room Occupancy, or SRO, was a ubiquitous, albeit thankfully vicarious, acronym in my early New York life. There were SROs in virtually every neighborhood in town, certainly every neighborhood I lived in. After college, I worked in a literary agency that had briefly dabbled in talent representation, and the occasional headshot still found its way over the transom. It amazed me at the time that almost every cover letter spoke of performing for "SRO audiences." I remember thinking—while fondly picturing Stage Door Canteen–like evenings of valiant thespians entertaining the borderline indigent with monologues from *The Glass Menagerie* or selections from the Harold Arlen songbook—*My goodness, I had no idea that New York's acting community was so civic-minded!* It wasn't until years later when someone pointed out to me that SRO also meant "Standing Room Only."

shift, drunkenly screaming "Fawkin' niggah!" at anyone who walked by, Madame Balzac would spend her time climbing the fire escape in back from room to room, quite naked. Whatever the weather, there she would be, the aging flaps and dewlaps of her raddled skin shuddering up and down the rusty iron ladders.

On the ground floor below me was an office that did . . . what, exactly? Résumés, taxes? I can't remember. What I do remember is the man whose office it was: Raul Rivas. That is his real name. Raul Rivas was knee-bucklingly handsome. Perhaps if my life had been different, had I been a hot girl with a driver's license, say, I might have put on a tube top and gone outside to wash my car in slow motion, dousing the cherry-red hood of my automobile in a spew of water from a long hose and then working it up into a suggestive and creamy froth, while Raul Rivas watched me through the open office door, sweating through his white undershirt, just like Burt Lancaster in *The Killers* . . . but, I digress.

Once during the day—it must have been a weekend because I was at home—I could hear Raul Rivas having sex in the office downstairs. I skittered around the apartment like a cockroach on a frying pan, trying not to make noise while desperately looking for a knothole in the crappy floorboards. Eventually I just lay down flat against the tile of the kitchen floor, listening.

Lying flat against the tile of the kitchen floor listening to someone else have sex is essentially my early twenties in a nutshell. I was robbed in that neighborhood twice—once by a fellow who asked me for all my money and when I demurred, showed me the gun in the waistband of his trousers while suggesting that I reorganize my priorities, and the second time when I blithely walked into the Laundromat to find the poor young fellow who gave out quarters sitting there, glum, mute, and at gunpoint. I wasn't remotely hurt in either instance (that honor was reserved for the tony West Village, where I had the shit beaten out of me one night by some toughs who, in the process, roughed up my copy of *Dombey and Son* and took my wallet—a largely value-less quarry back in the days before I had a credit card—and had to confine their criminal activities to taking books out of the library in my name and never returning them), but still, there were days when it hardly seemed worth it to live in a horrible part of town just so I could go daily to a stupid, soul-crushing, low-paying job. Especially since, as deeply as I yearned to be creative, for years and years I was too scared to even try. So I did nothing. But here's something I did do:

I paid my fucking rent.

It isn't that I don't sympathize with the lassitude. I understand it all too well. Creativity demands an ability to be with oneself at one's least attractive, that sometimes it's just easier not to do any-thing. Writing—I can really only speak to writing here—always, *always* only starts out as shit: an infant of monstrous aspect; bawling, ugly, terrible, and it stays terrible for a long, long time (sometimes forever). Unlike cooking, for example, where largely edible, if raw, ingredients are assembled, cut, heated, and oth-erwise manipulated into something both digestible and palat-able, writing is closer to having to reverse-engineer a meal out of rotten food. So truly, if you're already getting laid and have managed to fall in with an attractive and like-minded group without the added indignity of diving face-first into a cesspool every single time you sit down to work, no one understands bet-ter than I do why one might not bother.

The rude precariousness of this constant beginner-hood would be enough disincentive without the added mind fuck of how diametrically counter the creative trajectory runs to all other tasks. Among the multitude of reasons that it is better to be a grown-up than a child, just one is the mastery of the physical world. As a child, the distance between desire and execution was a maddeningly unbridgeable chasm. What the mind's eye pictured and what the body could achieve were altogether different: those stubby safety scissors could only ever cut an edge that was ragged and inelegant; glitter was invariably swallowed up into the pile of carpets as if by malicious intent, like Charlie Brown's grinning, kite-eating tree; the dried macaroni we were forced to incorporate into designs didn't have the decency to stay on the page, despite the glue getting everywhere (even at age four I understood this to be the lowest form, the operetta of visual art). Regardless of the medium, everything at that age ended up a muddy, crumb-flecked mess. In John Guare's play *Six Degrees of Separation,* the protagonist, Flan, says: "When the kids were little, we went to a parents' meeting at their school and I asked the teacher why all her students were geniuses in the second grade? . . . Matisses everyone . . . What is your secret? And this is what she said: 'Secret? I don't have any secret. I just know when to take their drawings away from them.'" Rather than a time of wonder and innocence, the all of it was a daily exercise in frustration and chubby-fingered inefficacy.

But then hands grow from smudging little mitts into useful instruments. The soup does not splash up over the rim, the glitter—should one ever be moved to use any—would stay where it was meant to. One progresses from novice to adept with a soothing reliability. Except for writing. Well into adulthood, writing has never gotten easier. It still only ever begins badly, and there are no guarantees that *this* is not the day when the jig is finally up.

And yet, I don't for a moment forget that this is not a life of mining coal, waiting tables, or answering someone's phone for a living. Each morning begins suffused with this sense of privilege, shell-pink and pulsing with new hope. The terrors and agitations of the night fade away and here it is, the clean expanse that is 6:00 AM, free of most everything but promise. Caffeination, evacuation, ablution, through all of which I spool out lovely and eloquent paragraphs in my head. And so to the gym where the lungs take in the new air, the fresh blood courses, and *look!* Here it is, barely 8:30. You'll be home and at your desk, scribbling away before other folks have even gotten to work! What grandiose hopes for the deathless prose that will be hoiked up from your depths, taking as evidence the sentences that flow easily through the mind as you do your crunches, the language graceful, propelled forward by the power of its own logic, a Slinky waterfalling effortlessly down a staircase. The toddlers of the day-care center next door are delivered. The carousing teenagers from the high school across the street deposit their cell phones and dime bags into the shrubbery by the stoop and line up for the metal detectors. The computer is turned on, opening up to the file left off the day before. *Today* will be good, you think. Not like the previous day's lack of industry, a shameful waste of phone calls, e-mail, snacking, and onanism.

Yes, it is all about today. But first, the crossword. And what does Paul Krugman have to say? Oh, that Gail Collins. *Love* her. E-mail, has it been checked in the last forty seconds? And now a snack. Friend Patty calls. She can't settle, either. Midday already? The toddlers, now screaming, are picked up from next door. Sit down and write a sentence for God's sake. One fucking sentence, it won't kill you. It almost kills you. Funny thing about words. Regarded individually or encountered in newspapers or books (written by other people), they are as lovely and blameless as talcum-sweet babies. String them together into a sentence of your own, however, and these cooing infants become a savage gang straight out of *Lord of the Flies.* A sullen coven with neither conscience nor allegiance. It will take the civilizing influence of repeated revision to whip them into shape, an exhausting prospect. Time for the late-afternoon power nap ("Ten minutes is all I need, and then I'm good for the rest of the day!" you brag to anyone who cares to listen). You rise, refreshed, your sense of creative optimism restored—or it would be if it wasn't for the maniac on the street crackling that cellophane wrapper. Who the *hell* does he think he is? Stand at the window and scan the sidewalk like a crazy person. Uh-oh, here comes that woman with her schnauzers again, animals that exist in a constant state of high barking dudgeon. Log on to that dog-breed website (again) to see how long the average life span is for such a creature. How much Xanax crushed up and mixed into some ground beef would it take to . . . never mind. Sit back down. And nothing. Whither flown the clarity of those morning insights? How many times must it be demonstrated to you that that interval of genius is as thin and fragile as the skin of an onion, if not downright illusory? And yet you never rush to the desk to get the pearls down on paper because in the moment of thought, they seem incapable of dissipation. So immortal, so solid in their reasoning, like those musings just before dropping off to sleep. *Why disturb this almost-slumber by writing? The Brooklyn Bridge doesn't crumble simply because one shifts one's gaze from it. Of course I'll remember something this obviously brilliant in the morning*, only to wake the next day without the remotest idea. Might as well finish eating that dried mango.

Oh, Google, how *does* one make soap?

The teenagers leave school, a good forty minutes of profanity (as comic genius Jackie Hoffman has observed, "It's all '*What the shit the fuck you are!*' And the boys are even worse"). The street goes quiet again. You can see the custodial staff cleaning the classrooms. The streetlights come on. They'd look so pretty against the sapphire of the early-evening sky if they didn't signify the hours you've wasted. If you were any kind of writer, you'd stay in and do battle, wrest the time back and make the day mean something more than the nothing it is turning out to be. But you are not any kind of writer. Today has proven as much. As did yesterday and odds are tomorrow will attest to the same. Pregnant with Potential has turned to Freighted with Failure. And so another day fails to meet its promise and has spun out into procrasturbatory entropy. You power down the computer. Just before the screen goes dark, the sentence you wrote chuckles and says, "Until tomorrow, maestro." Its tone is contemptuous, vaguely threatening, and deeply reminiscent of somebody's voice you can't quite place (three guesses whose). You will see friends and they will ask after your day and you will complain, charmingly (although not nearly as charmingly as you think), about what you haven't accomplished. Sometimes, it's just easier to go to dinner. Although, when you wake briefly at 4:00 AM in an anxious fury with yourself, you will know it is also exponentially so much more difficult to have gone to dinner.

The truest depiction of the writing life remains Nicolas Cage in the movie *Adaptation*, crippled by fear of inadequacy into near-complete inaction, opting to masturbate for the umpteenth time that day. His legs are the only thing visible on-screen, shaking, defeated, his off-camera body working its way to a sad and dribbling (anti)climax, the only thing he will produce the whole day.

And I understand, I really do. Who wants to hear a song about that?

It is never easy to publicly oppose something that achieves brilliant, unstoppable heights. It can make you seem bitter. I once ran into a friend and his mother at the movies. The subject of Philip Roth came up. (No surprise, really. We Jews are always talking about Philip Roth. We speak of little else, in fact.) It turns out my friend's mother had known him growing up in Newark. She was not a fan.

"Pffffft. Philip *Roth*," she spat. "He was such a jerk. I always wished him ill."

Well, good luck with that, I thought, as the lights went down.

We were at *The Red Shoes,* possibly the best movie ever made. Certainly one of the best movies ever made about what it means to be creative. Moira Shearer plays Victoria Page, a girl whose single-minded devotion to the ballet makes her a great star. Everyone loves Vickie and everyone wants to mold her to his own purposes: the multilingual ballet impresario with the silk dressing gown and pencil mustache; her husband, the composer. Finally, it is all too much for poor Vickie. Moments before she is to take the stage in Monte Carlo, she snaps, and in full ballet makeup—her mouth a red slash, her eyes darkly rimmed and extended like pointed black leaves—she runs from the theater, down the broad stone steps of the opera house, and flings herself over an ornate balustrade into the path of an oncoming train fifty feet below.

The greatest dancer of her time is gone. She has literally died for the art that, in life, consumed her constantly and completely. All is loss and sorrow. Still, the ballet of *The Red Shoes* goes on as scheduled, as it must, and in Victoria Page's stead, a lone spot-light, illuminating the places she *would* have been dancing. It is a fitting tribute, this bright absence, gliding across the stage. Because without the work, there is nothing.

The Satisfying Crunch of Dreams Underfoot

Scientist Stephen Jay Gould posited the theory of punctuated equilibrium, which contends that the earth's biota, rather than existing on a constant and linear march toward development and proliferation, can sometimes experience long stretches of evolutionary stasis, followed by irregular bursts of rapid and radical change.

There you are, for example, rooting for grubs in the dirt, pushing aside spongy logs with your ineffectual proboscis, as you and your ancestors have been doing for ten millennia, and suddenly everything changes and surges ahead with a charged developmental fury. The same time the next year, you're picking up fat and nutritious larvae between your highly dexterous forefinger and opposable thumb, all the while thinking, *Once I've developed agriculture, I'll dredge these in a little cornmeal and cook them over that fire I just invented.*

For most of us, life is a fairly steady trek, and such high-flown dreams of thumbs and cornmeal and fire are adaptive boosts we neither deserve nor could possibly hope to attain in our lifetime. The myth of the overnight success is just that. Only once did I find myself at the center of an evolutionary fluke of such gargantuan proportion as to confound even a genius like Stephen Jay Gould. One day a grunt in publishing, and the next ushered past the velvet rope into a whole new life. (*Allow us to help you down from that tree, Mr. Rakoff . . . We hope you enjoy your new upright posture, Mr. Rakoff . . . How about a bigger brain case, Mr. Rakoff . . .*) In such an exclusive world, it was a testament to the top-drawer quality of both that the jumbo shrimp and baby lamb chops should be the same size. The strawberries were as big as a newborn's head and the muffins appeared to have been baked in thimbles. Whole carrots were as slender as golf pencils and the water came in tiny glass bottles more traditionally used to hold ampoules of morphine. It was a Lewis Carroll buffet, the scale of everything either amplified or diminished to signify privilege, nothing more so than the fact that no one was eating, not even me. Not because I was blasé. I am never blasé about food, especially free food. I was not eating because I was nervous, standing in that small chandeliered room, about to sit down for a read-through of the screenplay for a movie that was to begin shooting. A movie in which I had been cast.

It was 1995, and I was still working full-time as a propagandist and in-house writer in the book trade. I wrote press releases and the occasional remarks for the publisher. I amused myself by peppering his speeches with ever-nellier references from my own life. It began subtly, but if my stealth campaign proved successful, by the end of the year, this married father of children would be welcoming the sales reps with breathless references to watching *La Strada* while smoking and crying in the balcony of the Paris cinema. It was an easy job and no one bothered me. It afforded me a paycheck, health insurance, an office and its attendant supplies (O glorious Post-its), and as long as I turned my work around quickly, a good deal of free time in which to do freelance writing assignments. I also very occasionally got to act in the odd downtown production with friends. The casting director of the film saw me in one of them, called me in for an audition, and I got the part. It was a big movie. A gynocentric comedy predicated on the scenario where men are cheating bastards and middle-aged women the goddesses who best them while cementing their sisterhood with Motown-scored makeover montages, vengeful shopping sprees, warmed-over Lucy-and-Ethel hijinks, and random humiliations visited upon women who are younger and therefore by definition stupid whores. It was based on a novel by an author published by my employer, coincidentally, about whom more later, except to say that we were friendly at one time but she might just be the only person in my entire life about whom I've said something purposely, gratuitously injurious and deeply unkind.

I was one of the few people in the room who was not known. There were three iconic female stars, a supporting cast of respected actors, and a fearsome producer with a talent for hits and a reputation as the devil incarnate. Not a room in which to be seen eating. My presence there would have been the classic Cinderella story if instead of being delivered from her grimy scullery to the carefree life of the palace, our dainty-footed heroine was a thirty-something guy who had left his evil stepsisters to go off and play a mincing fairy interior decorator. The Stepin Fetchit aspects of my part extended beyond the sexual to the ethnic. My part was that of an ersatz food-court Latin of indeterminate national origin. Even his name, Duarto, does not exist in Italian, Spanish, or Portuguese, a testament to the deep research for which our author was known. Snippy ectomorphs like Duarto have been a staple of the movies since the early talkies. You have seen us, I am sure. Generally, we are slim, our hair is often brilliantined and pasted down like a phonograph record molded directly to the skull. We have been known to sport the occasional eyebrow-pencil mustache. Our jobs tend toward the mildly creative and powerless—tango instructor, wedding consultant, Hays Office–approved neutered gigolo. Also, traditionally we exhibit two modes of behavior, both of them manifestations of displeasure. There is our comically outraged ethnic or sexual pride, the former eliciting from us a fiery Chiquita Banana *"You een-solt my cohn-tree?"* (which, as we have established, with a name like Duarto, does not actually exist and is therefore not really insultable), and the latter a dubiously macho defense of the molested honor of our woman, our own interest in whom would have to increase tenfold to reach the level of repelled. The far more common state of a Duarto, however, is one of peevish boredom and affronted aesthetics (*"Dios mío,* where did you get that *agonizing* side table?"). This makes us speak in a kind of enervated drawl that broadcasts to all the world that we would much rather be anywhere else than here, preferably somewhere holding a teacup poodle while being the willing recipient of vigorous anal sex.

And all of it with an accent. I based mine on that of a fellow with whom I went to college. It was 1982, and as best as I can remember, he majored in Peppermint Lounge, with a minor in Pyramid Club. If you asked him where he was from, he responded with, "I am from Europe. Okay, fuck you, Venezuela," which wasn't even true. He was Israeli.

The screenplay reading went well. In addition to Duarto, I was pinch-hitting for three small parts. People were extremely nice to me. I made Diane Keaton giggle at one point; Bette Midler and I talked about her daughter's school. Sarah Jessica Parker, Victor Garber, and J. Smith-Cameron took me for a post-traumatic drink at the Waldorf bar, and I walked home through the rain, tipsy and thrilled.

I had been granted admittance into a club I'd no right to be in. Somehow, despite my lack of formal training and my decidedly slim and exclusively off-off-off-Broadway résumé, the dues I'd paid in other realms—a bout of illness here, years logged in day jobs I didn't enjoy there (*can you imagine such suffering?*)—could be converted somehow and cashed in for a flight to this new and coveted realm. This role would lead to others and I would never have to go back to the publishing house. Certainly the folks on the movie made me think so. The director took me out for a drink one evening and, like new lovers who endlessly narrate the thoroughly unremarkable details of their early meeting that happened just three weeks prior, he and I fondly recapitulated the out-of-nowhere story of my being cast. My part was at best a cameo and they made me feel like the lead. I was drunk on potential fame. For the next few weeks, I led a double life that was cinematic itself, spending my days at the office but dashing off during lunch hours and evenings after work for rehearsal, makeup and hair tests, and wardrobe appointments—where I was outfitted in a pair of trousers so tight that it would not be until years later when I had a hemorrhoidal ligation that I would experience such constriction again. When principal photography finally began, I cashed in all my vacation days, thinking as I left the office, *I'll be back . . . To clean out my desk,* suckers!

My first day of shooting was out in Queens. I was given a trailer. Well, a slice of a trailer, the union-required minimum of space, called a honey wagon (which I would later find out is the term they use for those trucks that suck human waste out of septic tanks, which I would also find out isn't that odd a coincidence). We were filming a scene between Bette Midler and myself, set in my decorator's atelier. Duarto seemed to favor a maximalist aesthetic of paisley throws on overstuffed furniture, embroidered pillows, fat silk tassels, and garden urns. Bette Midler was bookish and friendly to the extent she felt comfortable being. We got along fine. That's not meant to damn with faint praise.

Quite the opposite. It's very strange to be around the visually famous. It must be tremendously difficult for those whose very faces make up an integral part of the landscape. Everyone wants something from them, even those people who would deny it, or don't know it themselves. Usually it's nothing more than to be seen by the celebrity. You're always conscious of where they are in the room. I once watched Jacqueline Onassis wait for an elevator, and the heightened performance of casualness of everyone around her paying her no notice had about as much in common with ignoring someone as a Father's Day department-store window resembles an actual barbecue. I had no illusions that what was, for me, a peak experience was for Ms. Midler just another day, and likely one she would never remember, if I could manage to get through it without vomiting on myself in public which, it turns out, there is more than one way of doing.

Things began promisingly, but as the day progressed, something felt slightly off. I was not used to camera acting and was unprepared for just how different it felt from being onstage: the lack of sequence, the fragmentation, the waiting around, the crew standing so close, and the equipment hovering just overhead. In addition to the tight pants, they outfitted Duarto with a scarf made of yards of fabric that swooped and draped in a series of folds around my neck. I looked like the setup of that old Isadora Duncan joke (*"Oh, wear the long one, dear. It'll bring out your eyes . . ."*). If we did a take, if I sat down, if I had a sip of water, the continuity person had to come over to adjust the drapery just so, to match the Polaroid they had taken earlier that morning. I became afraid to move and lost my coordination. At one point, as a bit of business during one take, I idly picked up a prop off my desk—a beautiful old artist's model of a hand, carved from honey-colored boxwood—and gestured with it.

The director liked it and instructed me to keep it in. But when I tried to do it again, I couldn't even find the object on my desk, finally fumbling for it and all of it looking incredibly forced. It only got worse. It was like poorly following a pattern for a shirt or a set of plans for a building. I was making small errors that compounded themselves so that by midway through the process, I had created a misshapen garment with three sleeves, a house with no door.

Apparently, I was the only one who thought so. The director seemed pleased, going so far as to tell me at lunch, "I think you have a future in film." I received similarly kind words from the horde of producers milling about—a cadre of young men on whom I had never clapped eyes before that day. We finished up, I returned to my trailer, unwound the scarf, and peeled off my tight pants. I almost passed out as half of my blood supply rushed precipitously away from my heart and brain and down to my legs. I changed back into my street clothes and stood on the curb outside the honey wagon and waited for the van back to Manhattan. Bette Midler's car drove up and stopped about eight feet away. I could see her in the backseat, studying the next day's script. The limo was long enough that her reading lamp did not disturb the driver. Her hair was wound up in a post-wig Nefertiti contraption, rising from her head like a soft bongo drum.

She'll see me standing here, I thought. *She'll tell her driver to open the door and I'll get in and we'll ride back to Manhattan, chuckling ruefully all the way about this crazy business. We will return to her rambling apartment. It will be the maid's night off and we'll eat leftovers from the icebox: cold chicken and pie. Milk from a glass bottle. Then I'll say, thinking out loud more than anything else, I'll say, "If only we could turn this into an all-singing, all-dancing musical picture." "Why that's a marvelous idea!" she'll exclaim. Then we'll stay up the whole night at the piano, working out a terrific bunch of socko numbers, catchy songs, and snappy dance routines!* But the Divine Miss M never glanced my way as her car drove off.

You know that old principle that says that wishing will not make it so, but stating your worst fears just might? Okay, it's not an old principle, I made it up myself, but only through direct and repeated observational proof. I have seen more times than I can discount where the verbalized worry that a spouse has had an affair was precisely both catalyst and fuel that resulted in the infidelity—the pile of rags, can of oil, match, and ready supply of pure oxygen, all in one. In my own life, I've scotched countless encounters by being far too vocal with my anxiety. I can't help myself. When I spoke to anyone connected with the movie, from the director or the producer, to my agent, to anyone with an unobstructed ear canal, truth be told, I always joked, "Have I been fired yet?"

So when my agent called me the very next morning, before I was to leave to meet the van back out to Queens, and said without preamble, "I'm sorry, my friend, you're off the movie," I jovially riffed with him for fully five minutes before I realized he was not joking. I once almost let a friend board a transatlantic flight without telling her that she had unwittingly tucked her dress into the back of her panty hose. In the end I took pity on her, but for the brief period before I did, it was exquisite to watch her walk around that way. It turns out to be somewhat less so when it is your ass that's poking out in the duty-free.

I might have seen the writing on the wall if I'd been anything other than a complete neophyte. Years later, I read a first-person account by an actor who claimed that it was common Hollywood knowledge that when someone tells you they think you "have a future" in the movies, as the director told me at lunch that day, the unspoken follow-up is understood to be "but not *this* movie." He told me at lunch. That means they already knew by noon that I was a terrible mistake. That they even let me continue with the afternoon's shooting seems, in retrospect, a courtesy. A few days later, the director sent me a kind note that read, "Dear David. I am very sorry, but as far as I'm concerned, you just had your reservations on the *Titanic* cancelled. You should look at it that way, too."

They replaced me with Bronson Pinchot.

I went back to my publishing job, weeks earlier than planned, although something like $9,000 richer. They paid me my entire salary. It was, up to that moment, the single largest sum I had ever received. I bought a sofa and a week in Italy with the money. It only occurs to me now that this windfall was undeniably classy on their part, but such a payoff also speaks eloquently to how fervently they wanted me gone and effaced with the kind of permanence that scours away any evidence of my ever having been there.

I was embarrassed to be off the picture, but not hugely surprised. The movies are full of examples of people getting fired for reasons having little or nothing to do with their performance. My story was hardly unique. Except I really kind of stunk. While I can be fairly amusing on stage and radio, on camera I had—at least back then—what might best be described as screen absence.

Being fired was an entirely new experience, and not because I was so good at the jobs I had held up until then, although I was a crackerjack secretary, if I say so myself. It's just that it was extraordinarily difficult to be fired in publishing. I don't mean being laid off, which is extraordinarily easy—the book trade has been in peril since Gutenberg—I mean to be seen as so incompetent that the unmitigated pain-in-the-ass alternative of training someone new for your $18,000-a-year job is considered preferable to your continued presence on the hallway.

The only indication I have that I must have felt humiliated returning to work is that I have no clear memory of it. It can't have been terribly pleasant to drag my vanquished self back to a job that was meant to supplement my creative urges, urges that had been shown to be delusional or, at best, validated in error and quickly corrected. There would be no punctuated equilibrium for me. I would not be advancing by undeserved leaps and bounds up the food chain, as I had hoped. I was back to my life of employing my crude, thumbless limbs and avoiding those predators bent on my devourment.

Such as the author herself. Before any of this happened, we were friendly. It started when she had been given my name as a source for repartee and anecdotes for a book she was in the process of writing: a potboiler roman à clef about publishing, for which she received more than a million dollars. She never failed to receive at least a million dollars for any of the books she wrote, the vast majority of which didn't come close to earning out their advances (this is not the unkind thing I said about her, that comes later . . .). We became friendly. She was a great deal of fun and unstinting in her generosity, standing me to a very fancy midtown lunch. She came to see me more than once in a play downtown, and when I was cast in the movie of her book, she took an almost maternal pride in my success. The commiserating phone call she made when I returned to work was entirely in keeping with the bond we had forged. But so was the subsequent turn of events, as relayed back to me later. According to her editor, I had, during our last call, bad-mouthed her and the movie, and told various lies about the director, the publisher, etc. I was made out to be a bitter, crazy loose cannon, and I was summarily dropped. This wasn't surprising. I had been warned from the beginning that she was a hot stove of a girl. Her path was littered with casualties—people with whom she had had intimate relationships who then couldn't get her on the phone, or found themselves on the wrong end of unkind gossip or scabrous misinformation with only one possible source. When things inevitably soured between her and her editor, for example, she reportedly sent him a bag of candy hearts, each one of which she had violently defaced with an alternate, vitriolic, and decidedly un-lovey-dovey message. I had gotten off easy.

Until came the day not long thereafter when we had to promote her characteristically terrible book (this, too, is not the unkind thing I said). Someone had the bright idea, since this was a novel about a character finding fame and fortune as a writer, that in a vain attempt at generating publicity for this book that no one cared about, and as a sop to her huge, unwarranted vanity (nor is that), we should have a literary contest in her name, calling for submissions of first novels, and we would publish the best one.

In the children's fairy tale *The Little Princess,* a young girl of noble parentage is orphaned and briefly laid low by circumstance, reduced to working as a common char under the thumb of an abusive schoolmistress. When the girl's nobility is eventually discovered and she is to be restored to her life of silks and velvets, she turns to her best friend—another soot-covered menial who labored in the house next door and who was the only person in the world who showed the princess any kindness—and asks her if she'd like to come with her to her new, palatial home . . . as her *maid*! The lowborn urchin, far from being insulted, replies in the gleeful affirmative. Because I am not a Victorian child inculcated from birth with the tenets and strictures of the British class system, I always told myself that, were I to find myself in a similar situation with just such a subjugation-posing-as-my-lucky-day-bonanza offer made to me, I would have both backbone and presence of mind enough to answer, "Your maid? I'd love to. Would you, in turn, like to suck my dick?"

But when told that it would fall to me to administer the contest—read all the submissions and choose a winner, in essence take on what amounted to another full-time job on top of the one I already had, and have to be back in touch with and even somewhat in the employ of the author, in whose eyes I was not just Box Office Poison but toxic to life offscreen, as well— my nerve failed me. I had no choice. I needed the job. They'd asked me to eat shit, and all I'd done was request a bigger spoon.

I consoled myself with the knowledge that we would receive very few entries, since the contest had been advertised on the back page of the very book we were trying to promote. A star-burst on the cover announcing the sweepstakes, even printed within the first few pages, seemed clever enough, but a promotion meant to drum up sales where the enticement was printed on the last page, a page generally only reached at the end of having read the entire volume, namely *after* one had already purchased the book and was by definition no longer in need of any further incentives or blandishments, seemed akin to handing out entry forms for a Caribbean cruise on the deck of a ship already three days out to sea.

But, lo and behold, mere days later, I started to get submissions. A trickle at first, they soon arrived by the binful. Over the course of the next three months or so, I received manuscripts for some two thousand first novels. I stacked them on a spare desk in my office. They covered its entire surface to a height of three feet, a daunting manila butte. The author came in to pose for a photograph for *Publishers Weekly*, seated among the piles of aspirants. The queen with her golden milk pail, she made a comically overwhelmed Teri Garr face, as if she had spent hours reading and had hours more still to go which, I hardly need to point out, she hadn't and didn't.

My days, however, were taken up with reading. For this aspiring writer who just couldn't seem to get his own writing done, there was more than a touch of humiliation in being faced with two thousand individuals who could, and cold comfort in the fact that a goodly handful of those industrious souls seemed to be either insane, incarcerated—or both. I might have chuckled with superiority when I read the manuscript that began, "Hello, I was in the Ice Capades in 1947 and let me tell you, everyone thinks that Sonja Henie was such a sweetheart but take it from me she was one unholy bitch on skates!" But I could not ignore the material rebuke that was the word-covered sheaf of pages, thick in my hands.

There was no way I would make the contest deadline, so I pressed three co-workers into service and we spent a few lunch hours a week going through the submissions. Particularly lurid or whacked-out passages cried out to be read aloud and chuckled over, but this was pretty much a busman's holiday for all of us. Publishing begins and ends with the reading of manuscripts. For the most part we ate our sandwiches and worked silently, all the while, of course, vigilantly on Devereaux Watch.

For mysterious reasons, possibly having to do with schlock auteur Aaron Spelling, in amateur writing, Devereaux is the default name for either the president, a ne'er-do-well scion of a powerful clan, an iron-willed jewel-encrusted dowager, or the family manse whose stately façade conceals many dark secrets. There was no prize for winning the Devereaux Watch. Coming upon the first—and by no means only—appearance of the name on a given day's reading was its own reward, and finding it never took longer than seven minutes.

Ha-ha! Aren't the doomed aspirations of others funny? Their pitiful lack of conversancy with this murky-yet-dreamed-of industry? A scream! Why, if I wanted to, I could have just walked my own manuscript downstairs to one of the editors. Where *was* my manuscript, you ask? Fuck you. When I wasn't awash in self-pity, I was as brittle and glittering and heartless as a shard of glass. Until the day I opened one of the submissions to read an epigraph of the poem that ends with the plea, "I have spread my dreams under your feet; Tread softly because you tread on my dreams." That shut me up but good, albeit for all of five minutes. William Butler Yeats might have had truth and beauty, but they were no match for my thwarted grandiosity. I had stepped off the career track, opting not to become an editor so that I might concentrate on my writing, of which I had produced a scant and laughable amount. Nor had I managed to make a go of acting, my other dilettantish pursuit. My contingency plans for a creative life were, one by one, failing to pan out, with nothing but a future of highly unromantic rent-paying ahead of me. If I had to eat so much failure myself, then by God, I'd be sure to mete some out, too.

We settled on four finalists, all of them very good, all eminently publishable: the first was an autobiographical novel of an Irish Catholic childhood destroyed by alcoholism in Greenwich Village in the 1930s; there was a terrific book set in the nineteenth century in the Five Points neighborhood, written years before the movie *Gangs of New York* came out; an extremely dark comic story of an obese man who finally snaps and goes on a killing spree that sparks a social revolution of fat people demanding fair treatment; and the winner, which was an assured and beautiful book about a family of Jewish refugees in the 1920s who move to South America. It was page after page of lovely writing, full of heat and Yiddish-inflected magic realism, an achievement of craft and virtuosity. Worlds better than anything the person for whom this contest had been set up could ever have written, even if she had taken a bottle of smart pills and was hooked up to an IV where she was getting hourly transfusions of liquid talent (injurious and unkind, perhaps, but still not the thing I said). This young woman would be published by the house, her dreams would come true, and it would shine the light of publicity upon our established author.

That had been the plan, anyway. By the time the contest was decided, however, the underlying book was already leaving bookshelves, having enjoyed dismal sales. There were no embers of interest left for the contest to fan into flame. The winner was published, but with little promotion and even less advertising. She was disappeared by this apathy, as unknown as if she'd never published a book at all. The entire enterprise had been ill-conceived and was, by the end of it, a desperate and resigned hookup in a bar at closing time with the lights turned up bright: exhausted, flailing, and tinged with contempt from and for all involved.

As for the other finalists, there would be no introductions to agents, no pictures in trade journals, no punctuated equilibrium of any sort. I was left to my own devices as to how to handle what had now officially become a problem that the higher-ups wanted taken care of. I walked over to Sam Flax and bought three ready-made frames with glass along with some oversized certificate-looking paper. I found some fancy gold-foil stickers in my craft drawer, and using an elaborate font, I mocked up an "official" citation. I mailed them off, feeling incredibly shabby about the whole thing. Then again, who am I to say what nourishes or starves a dream? When I called the fellow who'd written the Five Points novel to make sure the plaque had arrived, his wife told me that the validation of being a finalist had lifted him out of a years-long funk and he was writing again. I would never know, she told me, what a gift that was. She, in turn, would never know that the entire enterprise had been little more than a backfired prank, or that I was an over-entitled wage slave with absolutely no power and too wrapped up in my own aborted fantasies at the time to be of any help to anybody. And that the golden seals on the diplomas were salvaged from the packaging of the bathroom soap I bought in Chinatown for fifty cents a bar.

I never saw the author again. Not long after the contest, she found fault with the publishing company as a whole and moved on to more lucrative pastures. A few years after that, she went in for some plastic surgery and never came to, an untimely, wasteful, but thankfully probably painless end. Once, when leaving a party, my friend the hostess turned to a woman standing beside her—Upper East Side ash-blonde, black-velvet Alice band, gold Elsa Peretti earrings, pearl necklace—and said, "You should really meet David at some other time. He's very funny." The blonde looked me up and down appraisingly, and purred, "Yes, I bet I could have a lot of *bitchy* fun with you."

I could imagine which of my signifiers had led her to this conclusion. No doubt one of the visual cues I give off that had initially gotten me cast as Duarto. Whichever it was, I really didn't care, because with barely a pause between her words and mine, I corrected her, "Oh no. I *am* a homosexual, but I'm not a bitch." It was important to me that this woman I had never met know this. I value kindness in myself and others. I try to remain super-vigilant about my targets and make extra sure that my sometimes barbed comments are deserved and in response to some genuine malefaction. Perhaps my insistence on this nuance is waffling self-delusion, given what I have said in print about public figures like Barbara Bush, Robin Williams, and Karl Lagerfeld, to name just three. And what I am about to tell you—with no pride—weakens my claim to kindness to the point of pitiful. Before the author died and was lingering in a twilight of her anesthesia-induced vegetative state, the ether was a-crackle with a volley of e-mails from the legions to whom she had done dirt. All of us whose kindness she had repaid with cruelty could speak of nothing else. One of my former colleagues wrote:

"You'd have thought the doctors would get the ether right the first eleven times she had the procedure."

To which I replied:

"Do you think her being in a coma will affect the quality of her writing?"

Dark Meat

The chief rabbi of the shtetl, a sage renowned throughout the land as the greatest mind in Jewish thought, is approached by two young Seekers of Truth. They have traveled for weeks, a great distance, on foot, in order to sit at his feet.

"Rabbi," asks one, eager for wisdom. "Why can't we eat pork?"

The rabbi reels back and, smacking his hand to his forehead, exclaims, "We can't? Uh-oh!"

Purim commemorates the narrow escape from genocide of the Jews of ancient Persia. It is a great, collective *"Phew!"* of a celebration, a snatched-from-the-jaws-of-death festival, and as such, a holiday of heartily endorsed drunkenness: sanctioned inebriation to the point where one can no longer distinguish between Haman—the despised villain in the book of Esther—and Mordecai, the sanctified hero. Such codified abandon makes Purim replete with subversion. All manner of things forbidden throughout the year are not just allowed but called for on Purim: raucous noisemaking in the synagogue, costumes, carnivals. Purim is the one day of the year that the Talmud allows cross-dressing.

"There's a lack of reverence built into the holiday," says Rabbi X, the head rabbi of a sizable Reform congregation in a sizable American city, "so I thought to myself, what's *my* little rebellion going to be? For those twenty-four hours of Purim, I eat *treyf.*" Once a year, Rabbi X returns to the foods of his nonkosher youth ("I never saw my father happier than when cracking open a crab on the seashore"). Beginning at sundown the evening before, "I go to a place in Chinatown and eat this shrimp with special salt. Unbelievable. It's really a hole in the wall. The next morning is bacon and eggs at a diner. I don't mean this to be arrogant, but I'm recognized almost everywhere I go, so in the morning, I go to a totally out-of-the-way diner. Lunch is a pizza with double pepperoni and a Coke—to me, one of the finest combinations of food on the earth—and before sundown, always lobster. Lobster tails with drawn butter, at a little tourist place. The equivalent of going to Lowry's for the prime rib. It is clearly in contradiction to the letter, but completely embraces the spirit of Purim. And I'm a spirit-trumps-letter kind of guy."

There is a reason Rabbi X has opted for the pork products instead of, say, walking down the street in an Escada dress. His actions speak to a larger universal truth, and that truth is that between Jews and pork there is no greater love. Perhaps lacking the Darwinian elegance of the coevolution of humans and dogs, and undeniably one-sided—the scores of hogs who give their very lives so that *Hebreo baconophagis americansis* may continue to revel in the secular wonder of the BLT might have a thing or two to say about it, if only they could—but it is a great love, nonetheless.

The Old Testament forbids the eating of animals with cloven hooves or who do not chew their cud, or fish without scales, and of course, there is also that clause about not boiling a calf in its mother's milk. But it is fairly bare-bones in its instructions beyond that. The more tortuous rituals of *kashrut*—like the separate sets of dishes, what foods may follow others, the sanitizing of sullied implements by burying them in the dirt, etc.—are all later extrapolations of the Babylonian Talmud, the multivolume text of rabbinical commentary.

The Talmud is composed almost entirely of dispute, and the arguments were still raging several centuries later and many oceans away when, in 1885, a rabbi named Kaufmann Kohler authored a call for the modernization of American Judaism in a document that came to be known as the Pittsburgh Platform, Article 4 of which states: "We hold that all such Mosaic and rabbinical laws as regulate diet, priestly purity, and dress originated in ages and under the influence of ideas entirely foreign to our present mental and spiritual state. They fail to impress the modern Jew with a spirit of priestly holiness; their observance in our days is apt rather to obstruct than to further modern spiritual elevation."

This rejection of what was dismissed as mere "kitchen Judaism," had surely found fertile soil two years previously when, for the 1883 banquet of the graduating class of rabbis from the Hebrew Union College of Cincinnati, the menu included clams, shrimp, and frog legs. Now widely considered to have been nothing more than the mother of all caterers' errors, the mythology of the "*treyf* banquet" was taken up as a clarion call by the burgeoning Reform movement and such men as Kohler and his komrades.

Internecine disagreements among an interpretive rabbinate are emblematic of the interrogative nature of Judaism itself. We are a questioning people. Why shouldn't something as beyond-the-pale forbidden like the eating of pork become normative among people who fully and proudly identify as Jewish? It can be quite confusing to the outside observer to see Jews whose adherence to the laws of *kashrut* has all the logic and elasticity of quantum physics. Jen C., a freakishly gifted voice-over artist, able to switch from a guttural Queens housewife to a spot-on

Yoko Ono without even taking a breath, might have developed such versatility growing up in a "Conservadox" household. "My father came from an Orthodox background and my mother was Reform. But he wanted to maintain certain aspects of his Orthodoxy, so we were sent to super-crazy Orthodox yeshiva, but he also liked eating butterfly shrimp in Chinatown on Sunday night. At yeshiva, the worst thing you could possibly say was, 'I saw you eating a ham sandwich.' That was the ultimate bus taunt. We had a kosher home befitting any Orthodox Jewish family. The kitchen was kosher, *but* if the Chinese food was brought straight from the car to the coffee table in front of the TV and eaten on paper plates, then that was okay." This doesn't even take into account the C.s' all-bets-are-off "ConservaForm" beach house where anything went. "I remember I was five or six and I was telling my grandmother a story that somehow involved me eating a ham-and-cheese sandwich, and I remember thinking, 'Oh, that's not kosher,' so I changed it to a plain ham sandwich. She was horrified and I quickly said, 'No, no! It wasn't ham, it looked like ham but it wasn't!' I was covering."

A Red-diaper baby, raised according to the precepts of good old-fashioned pinko socialism, becomes an entertainment lawyer, successful enough that he can afford to send his son to that august private institution, the Trinity School on Manhattan's Upper West Side. One day, the man's eight-year-old son comes home and says, "Dad, we learned about the name of our school today. It's called Trinity because there's the Father, the Son, and the Holy Ghost."

Horrified, the father grabs his son by the shoulders before he can continue and, shaking him, says vehemently, "Joshua, get this straight: there is only one *God! Who does not exist!"*

For other, more progressive Jews, religiosity in all its opiate forms was anathema. The modern dispensation of the Pittsburgh Platform was no different from, nor any more attractive than, the dusty pages of the Talmud with its incomprehensible and inapplicable Aramaic. Both smacked uncomfortably of the clergy, and neither was going to bring about justice or help create a new society, of which *treyf*-eating was one demonstrable aspect.

It's hardly a maverick position to take; any revolution that includes a good carbonara is an awfully easy rampart to storm. It certainly helps that pork chops are so delicious, just one of the heavenly foods that come from what Homer Simpson calls "a wonderful, magical animal." But that's not the whole story. Attendant to all of this is the politically romantic and also very real notion that every part of a pig "but the squeal," as they say, can be eaten and used. Pigs have sustained countless cultures throughout history. The proletariat-nourishing utility of the pig made it the ideal animal for fiery young utopians (back before such activism also comprised the emancipation of other species). Pork served as the ultimate demarcation from the hidebound small-mindedness and superstition of the shtetl. Let Him show Himself and strike them down for eating *treyf*, if He was so g.d. tangible. Jewish radicals of the Bundist labor movement used to hold Yom Kippur Balls. The gatherings featured music; dancing; mocking Yiddish parodies of Kol Nidre, the penitential prayer at the heart of the holiest day in the Jewish calendar; and most transgressively, food. One such ball in 1890, organized by Russian Jewish anarchists in Philadelphia, was to pointedly include "pork-eating." At the eleventh hour it was called off, in deference to Sabato Morais, that city's Orthodox rabbi who had that year successfully mediated a strike by the cloak makers. In his Holo-caust memoir, *I Shall Live,* Henry Orenstein reminisces about how before the war in his Polish town a small but vocal contingent of "nonbelievers," no more than fifty, would commit the ultimate sin by eating pork on Yom Kippur. Every autumn, the gentile butcher, Mr. Krasnapolski, would ask the author, "Tell me . . . when is it, this day of the year when Jews are allowed to eat ham?"

Here would probably be a good place to say a brief word about crustaceans because, with the possible exception of the Cajuns, no one loves shrimp as deeply or as truly as the Jews (almost nothing fills me with a twingier regret than my recently determined allergy to the creatures). But the avid consumption of shellfish has its relatively recent roots in the New World Jewish habitat of the beach, and the country-club-striver weddings of the PhilipRothoisie. Among the many tenets of *kashrut,* it is the proscription against pork that sticks in the mind, for both Jews and Gentiles. Shellfish is nowhere near as freighted as pork. Many a Dungeness devotee would never dream of touching swine. Rabbi X has a colleague, also a prominent and respected cleric, who explains himself with, "I'll eat shrimp. No Jew ever died refusing to eat shrimp. But pork, never. Shrimp is *treyf,* but pork is anti-Semitic."

True enough. When I try to look up jokes about Jews eating pork, I am directed to an embarrassment of neo-Nazi sites, each boasting an exhaustive page of racist humor, with comic gems like: "Why don't Jews eat pork? Because the Bible forbids cannibalism." In a few keystrokes, I find myself at another website called www.nukeisrael.com ("exposing the Zionist lobby"), which has a page titled "Jewish Stars Over Hollywood: A look at the hundreds of filthy heb [*sic*] swine that control the U.S. entertainment business," listing noted Hebrews like Ellen DeGeneres, who I think is a nice Christian girl from Metairie, Louisiana, and Allen Ginsberg, who probably never set foot in a movie studio in his life and whom they identify, despite his mongrel-hood, as the "all time greatest American poet."

And yet, with all of this, I almost never feel more Jewish than in that moment just before I am about to eat pork. Allow me to horrify kosher readers when I draw a parallel between that instant and the custom of the breaking of a glass at a Jewish wedding, the perfect illustration of the Jewish worldview. In this somber evocation of the destruction of the Second Temple in 70 A.D. is a reminder that all joy houses the Newtonian capacity for an equal and opposite sorrow. As a Jew Who Eats Pork, extolling the boundless perfection of the baby pig at NY Noodletown at the corner of Bowery and Bayard necessarily requires a simultaneous split second of silent acknowledgment along with my blithe rhapsody that this is meat ineluctably bound up with my grim history. Otherwise, I'd just be a guy eating pork.

Granted, the Judaism I feel connected to has always been more cultural than religious, but both are predicated on a spirit of dissent, of voluble, welcome disagreement, and an institutionalized and fiercely protected duty to question authority.

(*Forgive me, one more: A grandmother playing with her five-year-old grandson on the beach is horrified when a wave comes up and swallows the child whole, dragging him out to sea. Falling to her knees, she addresses the heavens in a state of near hysteria. "Oh God, please return my beloved grandson to me and I will be your devoted supplicant forever and always." Her entreaty heard, the sky spontaneously clears, a second wave washes up on shore and belches forth the child, returning him unscathed, dry even. The grand-mother, elated, faces the horizon once more, and says with the merest trace of impatience, "He had a hat!")*

We are all enfolded, from the protest-too-much anarchists of the nineteenth century at their Yom Kippur Balls, up to the present day with our ever-growing ranks of Buddhists, even including, heaven help us, Republicans (who really ought to know better). We are all Jews. We are the true Big Tent. It is this that I taste: the fact that I do not have to be "on the bus." I can, in fact, stand by the side of the road with a sign that says DOWN WITH BUSES!—or, more authentically phrased: BUSES? FEH!—and still be able to claim full and proud membership. Which I do, emphatically.

Even when it is an identity foisted upon me by others. A few years back, my first book was translated into German and I was flown over for a tour. I don't kid myself: the primary reason for their interest in me was precisely because I am Jewish, our extirpated culture being somewhat fetishized in Germany today. I was a phantom talisman, like an ivory-billed woodpecker will-ingly visiting the strip mall that used to be his swampy habitat, or the walking illustration of that rueful old joke about the sub-urbs being the place where they chopped down all the trees and then named the streets after them. I spent a week as a Profes-sional Jew.

The fetishization cut both ways. With as much Stockholm syndrome as the next guy, I am not without my own febrile fan-tasies of racial purity and historical redress (known in the com-mon parlance as a Thing for Blonds). My friend Dan, Catholic but with the handsome Black Irish dark hair and eyes of a hot yeshiva student, filled my head with stories of his many con-quests when he lived in Berlin. Conquests he didn't even have to work at. Apparently the merest possibility that they were bedding down for some restitutionary, penitential face-sucking with a genuine Jewish American boy had German men throwing themselves at him. My charms, such as they were, seemed more historical than erotic. The Germanized Yiddish I spoke to make myself understood to hotel clerks and taxi drivers was met with what can only be described as delight, and a kind of wistful nostalgia for a time no one really remembered anymore, which invariably led to the time none of them seemed capable of forgetting. Every conversation I had began precisely the same way: "How does it feel for you to be here?"

I told them that I was very happy to be in Germany, and indeed I was, although a distinct impediment to comfort never left me, as if I were spending my time walking in shoes of slightly different heights. In the Berlin Zoo, for example, even I, who could not be described as an animal lover, was unnerved by attitudes that seemed to have been barely updated since 1844, when they opened the place. The enclosures and structures were small, rickety, and archaically anthropomorphic. The animals were housed like the humans of their respective countries, the prey adopting the customs of the local predators. The wild boars lived in a small thatched cottage, much like the people who hunt wild boars might have had in the Vienna Woods. The rams made their home atop a fake mountain in a little Tyrolean cabin with latticed windows. It looked just like the kind of place where Heidi and her grandfather might have lived, if Heidi and her grandfather had been curly-horned ungulates who shit indiscriminately all over their *schloss*.

Strangest of all, however, was the fur rug on the floor of the vulture cage. I swear it, a fur rug in shades of mottled brown and gray with a deep, ragged, sexy pile that Barbarella might have favored. It seemed an odd choice for an outdoor space, especially an outdoor animal enclosure. Approaching the bars, it became clear that this luxurious carpet was actually a large pile of dead rats and weasels. Some caring zookeeper had pre-killed a multitude of the critters, thoughtfully splitting them open from stem to sternum. A bald-headed bird eyed me casually as he picked at one of these rodent tacos. Giving his beak an upward jerk, a tenacious rat tendon stretched and finally snapped: the bored cashier with her chewing gum.

Morally neutral and completely natural though the food chain may be, and perhaps I'm overestimating the fame of Art Spiegelman's masterpiece *Maus*, where the Jewish mice were represented as precisely the vermin the Nazis described them to be, but I can't help feeling that if *I* ran the zoo—to quote Dr. Seuss—especially the Berlin Zoo, I would be extra careful about not leaving a pile of corpses lying around.

I take the U-Bahn, the efficient (duh) subway out to Hallesches Tor, to the Jewish Museum or, as it seems to be known, Architect Daniel Libeskind's Jewish Museum. All around the basement level, which is a series of off-kilter hallways dedicated to the Holocaust, are small notice cards printed with explanation for why Architect Daniel Libeskind designed things in the way that he did. Statements along the lines of, *As you travel the Axis of Exile, Mr. Libeskind hopes that through disorientation comes insight.* His desire to justify his choices seems reasonable: this was a lucrative and very public gig. But the thinking behind the oddly funhouse atmosphere down here is completely opaque to me. I'm hard-pressed to see why the Holocaust needs to be gussied up with corridors from *The Cabinet of Dr. Caligari*. It's fairly terrible and gripping all on its own. And there's a creepy celebrity-chef quality to Libeskind's omnipresence. *Mr. Libeskind hopes you can detect the top note of Tahitian vanilla in the beef cheeks with razor-clam foam.*

Libeskind might have saved the architectural bells and whistles for the upper floors, which cover the roughly thousand-year history of the Jews in Germany before the late unpleasantness of the 1930s and '40s. The display about what keeping kosher means, for example, could have used a little spice, although I do come upon an interesting interactive display: a computer with two large buttons: green for "Yes," red for "No." On the screen is the question: "Do you think it is all right to tell a Jewish joke in Germany today?" I'm assuming by "Jewish joke" they mean a joke told *about* Jews, i.e., "Knock, knock, who's there? Usurer," as opposed to a joke told *by* Jews, like I have done here, and will continue with *these* two, both of which were originally told to me by my Jewish parents, and both of which involve medicine and long-term-care facilities for the aged, which solidifies their Semitic bona fides beyond any doubt:

A doctor in an old folks' home is visited by his patient Max Goldfarb, ninety-two years old. Max has come for his checkup and to announce that he is about to be married to fellow resident May Koussevitzky, age eighty-nine. The doctor says to him, "You know, Max, I don't feel this is a violation of doctor-patient privilege because you're going to marry her, but I've examined May Koussevitzky and I have to tell you she has acute angina," to which Max responds, "You're telling me!"

Here's the second joke: *Two psychiatrists meet on the street and say hello. "How are you?" asks one. "Eh, not so good," says the other. "I had a stupid misunderstanding, a slip of the tongue. I was visiting my mother out at the old folks' home. We were having lunch and I asked her to pass me the salt, but instead I said, 'You fucking bitch you ruined my life.'"*

It's not that I hadn't been mightily impressed with the honesty that I'd encountered while there. The explanatory text at the house at Wannsee where the Final Solution was first drafted, and at some recently excavated bunkers where the SS conducted torture on dissidents, was written exclusively in German. These were not displays of contrition for my benefit. But jokes? I just wasn't sure. We still didn't seem thick enough on the ground for the familiar contempt of jokes, so I pressed "No." The computer told me the tally so far: 76 percent of those who responded agreed with me.

I experienced only two moments that might be described as fear and they were not even Jewish in nature: one when the ice-blue-eyed German shepherd that lived near the reception desk of my Berlin pension showed up, unaccompanied and growling, outside my door, and the other in a brick-vaulted rathskeller in Cologne when a group of football-jersey-wearing men broke into very martial-sounding, beer-soaked song. Maybe it was the claustrophobia-inducing basement aspect, because the spontaneous male chorus that erupted one evening in Munich in a famous beer garden didn't faze me. The garden, at the foot of a huge pagoda in a huge park in the middle of the city, was apparently Hitler's favorite, and even that seemed harmlessly distant. Sitting with my German publisher, I drank a pale, lemony beer in a tall trumpet of a glass, and ate a *Schweinshaxe,* a Renaissance-looking joint of silky pork with crackling skin.

After supper, we walked through the park to the nearby Haus der Kunst, a massive museum with brutalist columns, a building erected for Hitler. It was in the Haus der Kunst that the Nazis opened the three-year-long exhibit of degenerate art, a show that essentially included every major movement of modern painting and sculpture: the cubists, the expressionists, you name it. If it wasn't a painting of some Rhineland mountainscape with billowing Wagnerian clouds and a mighty stag in the foreground, or else a sanctioned portrait of *der Führer* himself, chances are it was considered the physical manifestation of the decayed morals of a subhuman race.

But that night, in a bit of wry symmetry the Reich would have shuddered to contemplate, *I* was giving a reading. The Jewish homosexual writer: the ultimate degenerate. I was welcomed without reservation despite the history, *because* of the history that lay thick as incense in the air and escaped no one's notice, neither mine nor my hosts'.

In his highly entertaining cultural history of the Yiddish language, *Born to Kvetch*, Michael Wex shows how Yiddish "arose, at least in part, to give voice to a system of opposition and exclusion." Jewish language and, by extension, Jewish culture was, perforce, based in a disdain for Christians, a disdain born of some very legitimate fear and mistrust. "Eating *treyf* signals a cessation of disgust for the Gentile world," says Rabbi X.

Eating pork, then, is a Jewish joke I feel licensed to tell. Unlike most subversive humor, though, it doesn't have its roots in transgression, at least not for me, while for one friend, a woman well into her adulthood, it decidedly does. Yet she eats it with gusto and frequency. She still feels that she is getting back at her mother with each bite, much like the Shangri-Las and their defiant love for the Leader of the Pack. This is what is known as an underlying motive, and I would respectfully submit that she would have neither the words nor the tools to understand such things if Jews *hadn't* begun eating pork, psychoanalysis and the interrogation of the unconscious being just one of the many exciting things with which newly secular nineteenth-century Jews replaced religion in their quest for greater existential meaning. No longer confined to narrow lives defined solely by liturgy, they were free to pursue all manner of spiritual fulfillments, filling their time with street theater, socialism, anarchism, movies, and jazz.

I know bacon has become something of a ubiquitous cliché of late ("a little too pleased with itself," as my friend Patty says), but when I eat a piece, aside from its preposterous, heart-stopping deliciousness, I taste all of that: all those years and all those migrations that brought me to that museum in Munich, to that privileged place in space and time. I taste Max Beckmann lithographs, Freud case histories, Emma Goldman exhortations, the tunes of Irving Berlin and his Tin Pan Alley chums. Just behind the bacon's bracing jolt of salt and its comforting embrace of fat and smoke, even more than its shattering crispness and tenacious, leathery pull, I taste the World.

On Juicy

Bomb Shelter was designed to teach us nuance and compromise; a welcome departure from the usual bombast of the *Bosses-Bad, Workers-Good, Kibbutz-Best-of-All* indoctrination of Socialist summer camp. A game of musical chairs with lethal consequences, the counselors would dress up as characters vying for salvation and we campers would make our selections for the limited places in the hypothetical bunker (in the summer of 1976, the premise still seemed entirely plausible). Each candidate was a flawed archetype: Construction Worker was young and strong and able to sire offspring, but he was also a meathead; Old Philosopher might have been the ideal choice for spiritual leader of the New World Order, but his advanced years meant that he was frail and probably shooting blanks; Young Woman, her obvious fertility notwithstanding—she was sporting an advanced pregnancy of a sofa cushion under her peasant blouse—lacked education or abilities . . . You get the picture.

Their presentations made, the contenders then walked around the room to address each team directly. It was like the Iowa caucuses if the Iowa caucuses had been attended solely by Jewish children with a collectivist bent from Canada. When we asked Chaya, the drama counselor who was portraying Aging Schoolteacher—very smart but old, barren, and weak—how she proposed to teach in a post-nuclear world bereft of school supplies, she answered with a vehement, "I can fashion pencils from twigs!" This struck us all as somewhat desperate. One should want to escape the fiery apocalypse, certainly, but one shouldn't be seen as actively *campaigning* for it. That was just vulgar.

Young Woman approached and I, elected team spokesman, voiced our concern that she seemed too tiny for safe childbirth in the hospital-free moonscape of the future. It's such an odd thing for us to have focused on, since we were all similarly small-boned. Moreover, it seems unsporting that we should suddenly hold Young Woman to the physical standards of genuine adulthood, given the pretend nature of the exercise. It was like doing an ultrasound of her "belly" and being troubled that her fetus appeared to be made of foam, or asking Old Philosopher how he planned to stay geriatric once he ran out of baby powder for his hair. How did a bunch of kids even know about pelvic width or childbearing hips, anyway?

Young Woman's face got suddenly sad. She put her hands on my shoulders and leaned her face into mine. I thought she was going to kiss me but her lips bypassed my cheek until I felt her mouth, hot against my ear. "Don't tell anyone," she whispered. "But I had an abortion last winter."

An abortion! Can you even imagine the lubricious thrill of being the recipient of such a disclosure? I am here to tell you that you cannot because its pleasures were unquantifiable. *If she had an abortion, then that meant . . . she wasn't a virgin!* I couldn't choose a favorite posy from this bouquet of penny dreadfuls, it was almost too much. And still, all I really wanted to do was to put my own hands on Young Woman's shoulders and look her in the face and snap her back to the reality of this artifice, back to this game. "Hey," I would say to her, "I am *eleven*!"

That Young Woman should tell me her secret was momentous, to be sure, but only in degree, not kind. This was an absolute jewel of adolescent *Go Ask Alice* reality; far and away the juiciest thing I'd ever been told up to that point (it was also just about the last time that I would characterize someone else's secret as "juicy." The word would eventually be stricken from my lexicon, about which more later), but by that age, I was already long established as the person to whom people poured out their hearts. I cannot remember a time when they didn't. As faggy, loud, skittish, neurotic, caustic, and polymorphously, fun-ruiningly phobic as I was (and boy, was I ever), the most striking thing about me was my size. I was the very opposite of a threat. If others had reservations about trusting me, they seemed to dissipate as quickly as that fleeting moment where one hesitates before undressing in front of the dog. I was there, but not really. In Gypsy folklore, when one has a secret that can no longer be borne in silence one digs a hole in the ground and speaks those terrible truths into it. I was that hole. But a hole with a difference. A hole who could arrange his features and posture into an expression that was simultaneously neutral and curious, but not morbidly so. A hole who knew enough, once confided in, not to be a malicious blabbermouth.

I don't know when I learned to do this, but I do know how. Psychiatry is the family profession. A certain kind of active listening and an understanding of the importance of confidentiality is just part of the fabric of many shrink households, just as Chinese immigrant homes might speak Chinese. It was understood that secrets exist for reasons. Reasons we sometimes would never know, but that still had to be honored, nonetheless. In some unspoken way, I had hung out my shingle from an early age and made it known that I was open for business. And I've been relatively lucky in the secrets that have been sent my way. Not because they are so juicy (again that awful word; I'll get to it, I swear) but because they are so relatively tame, in the larger scheme of things. I have never been told any tales of serious financial malfeasance. (No surprise there. I can imagine it would hardly be worth dealing with what would surely be idiotic but inevitable interruptions of "Wait, is 'net' the bigger number, or is that 'gross'?") No one has tearfully confessed to me an indiscretion involving, say, a blinding fugue state of racial hatred, a machete, and the innocent Tutsi children next door. There are perpetrators and victims aplenty in my closely guarded blotter, but no actual crimes committed, at least not in New York State. Most of what I hear about is infidelity. A lot of infidelity. So much infidelity it's a wonder anyone manages to stay together.

But together we are, enmeshed in an ever-more refracting web. As my friend Rebecca says, "We're all connected by paychecks and body fluids." My childhood dream—that I would move to New York and have a creative life filled with many interesting friends who had terrible, terrible problems—came true. New York is for me, at this point, almost shtetl-like in its overlap. I sat at a dinner with a friend and her parents as it slowly dawned upon me that the patriarch was none other than the man who had been habitually sleeping with (and slowly breaking the heart of) a man I knew who had a thing for older married guys who liked to wrestle. Another time, I mentioned to someone that some other friends I knew had a similar artwork in their apartment only to realize that *this* copy had been a gift—a token of philandery—from one of them. On one of my birthdays, with no plans of my own, I hung up from a phone call with a friend I was comforting in order to answer my buzzer, to find the straying, soon-to-be-ex-husband weeping, coming up my stairs to give me the same news. Still another weeping husband—I had hopped on the train to the Upper West Side from Brooklyn one Sunday morning because it had sounded on the phone like he might kill himself—forgot about me and left me in the bedroom while he called his wife, traveling on business, from the living room to confess all. He found me asleep on their bed four hours later. That was fun.

I've only ever gotten in trouble once, and then for a relatively minor infraction. I was silent about a friend's impending divorce, and another friend was angry with me for not having shared the information. I suppose it would have cost me nothing to have told all I knew, but if you fancy yourself a practitioner of discretion, you might as well try being discreet, no? Moreover, when I was called to be given the news—news I already knew, news I had chosen not to share, news about someone's very real pain—my friend's voice was almost musical, swooping with the italics of schadenfreude. "Want to hear something *juicy?*"

Here I will refer an old Yiddish parable: An old woman is called out of her house to join her neighbors in the fun of watching the village idiot ranting in the square. She goes, and there he is, a grown man, raving like a lunatic, spewing saliva-flecked curses at the crowd, who are all hugely amused, with the exception of the old woman, who doesn't crack a smile. "If he wasn't *my* idiot, I'd laugh, too," she tells them. This, then, is "juicy's" toxic bit of transubstantiation: secrets turned into gossip; your pain into someone else's pleasure. Every hilarious town fool is someone's schizophrenic son. So my answer to that question "Want to hear something juicy?" is almost always no.

One need employ no tricks in the getting of information, no special child-of-psychiatrist lingo, hypnotic gestures, or pendulous swinging of a pocket watch in front of people's faces. I don't wheedle. For the most part, I stay silent. I don't flatter myself. It requires no talent to get information, although it takes some skill to guard it. And I do guard it.

"You're a big ear," said a friend.

A big ear with a peppercorn for a heart. Like many impulses of an apparently altruistic cast, it was initially powered by a generator of unattractive self-interest, churning away in my grimy subbasement. By age eleven I understood that whatever deviant desires and inappropriate-object choices already roiling away in my young psyche (Edward Fox in *The Day of the Jackal*, Christopher Gable in Ken Russell's *The Boy Friend*, Rudolf Nureyev, just for juvenile starters . . .) might be best left un-broadcast until such time as I could, say, grow up and move to Manhattan. There is no better way to conceal oneself than by listening to others.

That's a tad cynical. Let me add that there is also, perhaps, no greater kindness. Plain old listening is the most basic therapeutic model. Even when its motives are of dubious purity, it can be tremendously helpful. For the auditor, however, years of attentiveness—and years of appreciation for that attentiveness—can have a detrimental effect, skewing self-perception, fomenting arrogance, and spawning dreams of a grand and entrepreneurial nature; tainted fantasies, for example, of monetizing an activity already managed as unthinkingly as breathing. And so:

The informational meet and greet about becoming a life coach was being held at a hotel hard by Grand Central. Despite a renovation a few years back—new surveillance cameras trained on the doors of the men's room just off the lobby, and the regular patrolling of security into the gents' to inquire of those fellows deemed to be lingering too long at the urinals—and notwithstanding a handsome interior of plasterwork, brass, marble, and thick carpet, the premises could not rid themselves of an illicit feeling of furtive transience.

That tentative legitimacy extended to this evening. I had recently seen a calendar of breast cancer survivors where every artfully draped playmate who had survived that dreaded disease was now a life coach. Really, how hard could it be?

A small group of fifteen or so had gathered in a thin slice of grandeur of a room. Chopped down in size two times, with front and back walls of corrugated, retractable louvers, the crystal chandelier illuminated a space not much bigger than a bedroom. The prospectuses were in their cardboard folders, fanned just so on the trestle table by the chuffing percolator, the Mint Milanos were stacked in their fancy paper ruffs. We stood around in our damp coats, most of us clearly weighing whether we should just leave before things began in earnest. A freezing rain had turned it into the kind of night where one wants to be home already.

Undaunted, the organizers—a sweet married couple in their sixties, New York Jews transplanted to Florida—moved through our awkward knot of wet wool and briefcases, introducing themselves, handing out cups of coffee along with glossy information packets, and inviting us to take our seats.

They began their pitch. "Therapy deals with what hurts. Coaching deals with what *works*," which conformed to what I'd heard derisively said of coaching: that it was essentially dumbed-down therapy for those people too proud or blocked to admit they needed it (also known as men). Opening aphorisms aside, it became clear that it was far less easy to become certified than we had all hoped. Basic training requires well over a hundred hours of instruction and study, which is heartening for those folks who seek out coaches for their problems, but disappointing to those of us looking to make a quick buck. Speaking of bucks, it cost around $3,000 just for the fundamentals. On the "th" sound in "thousand," before the word had been completely formed by the wife of the duo, one woman stood up and walked out without any ceremony. It looked like a possible exodus when the only other remaining woman stood up at the same time, but it was only to ask a question, and by ask a question, I mean make a declamatory pronouncement. It was not immediately clear whether she was there to learn how to become a life coach, came to find one for herself, or had just stumbled in off the street. Rising to speak seemed an oddly formal gesture in so small a room.

"Yeah," she began, sounding a little angry. "My name is Johanna." She sidebarred almost immediately, putting the organizers on notice that she was having trouble with how elitist the whole enterprise of life coaching seemed to her, but that's not why she stood up. "My problem is clutter!" She turned her head around to look at those of us sitting behind her, which was everyone as she had parked herself in the front row. She gave a low chuckle and a simultaneous look that was darkly amused and sexual. Johanna said it again, for emphasis, "Clutter!," and then chuckled once more, too. *You* know *what I'm talkin' about.* We didn't. She sat down.

Once they had gone through the details of the lengthy protocol—the weekly teleconferences, the one-on-one mentoring sessions, the various levels of apprenticeship and supervision before we would receive accreditation or clients of our own—they introduced their protégé, a newly certified coach and high-end residential real-estate agent in the Orlando area. He was a gay man of a sleek, bronzed, and slightly cheesy perfection native to the warmer parts of these United States. His enthusiasm for coaching was a whole-body affair, right down to his nipples, which poked through the clingy, cigarette-smoke-gray fabric of his sweater like a pair of distant headlights approaching through a bank of fog.

It was quite clear from the widespread fidgeting and watch-checking that not one of us here would go through with this. Aside from the fact that it was expensive, we were surprised and regretful to find the training process both time-consuming and legitimate. And although there would be no classes to attend in person—both our apprenticeship and the eventual treatment of our future clients would all be done over the phone from the comforts of our homes in our underpants, if we so chose—it was not enough to persuade us to sign up. It was just too many hours. I could imagine my ear after all that teleconferencing: hot and achy, the phone receiver as greasy and used as a pizza box.

"Any questions?" the woman of the couple asked. There were none. What had seemed so promising just ninety minutes ago when we all filed in—a quick stop on the way home from work to start on a whole new way of life—turned out, like most things in this world that are worth doing, to require effort; almost as much as training as a therapist, working with what hurts. We would just have to content ourselves with the trust of our friends as payment.

People began to gather up their briefcases and put on their raincoats. Many of them still had long commutes ahead of them. We left Johanna there. She had fallen asleep, her head thrown back, her mouth open, no doubt enjoying some well-deserved respite from the oppressive clutter that awaited her at home.

Present-day Toronto is a megalopolis of sprawl, but thirty years ago, it simply ended at Steeles Avenue, like a medieval map. On one side were apartment buildings, the last outposts of civilization, and right across the street, an unknowable expanse of open corn-fields stretching out to farming communities and farther away still, the vast, piney wilderness: bears, moose, eventual tundra, right across the road.

The winter after Bomb Shelter, Young Woman and I were pressed into service one Sunday to lead an afternoon program for children who lived north of the city. Yuval, the *shaliach*—literally "envoy," a kibbutznik sent with his family to live among us and extol the Socialist dream—drove us far beyond Steeles to an old one-room church of dull pink brick, standing in a treeless yard. We waited in the carpeted basement for forty-five minutes, chatting among ourselves, while not one child came. I can't imagine what we managed to talk about. Yuval was a man of forty with children, Young Woman was in university in the sciences, and I was all of twelve. I remember feeling like Yuval was cramping my style. Young Woman and I hadn't seen each other for more than six months; we had some catching up to do. She would no doubt be itching to bring her most trusted confidant up to speed on all that had transpired in her life.

After an hour with nobody having arrived, we decided to cut bait and head back to the city. Yuval would turn out the lights and lock up while Young Woman and I went outside to wait. We stood in the churchyard under a dull oyster-colored sky. The early-March air had the aspirin smell of winter trees and cold mud. I turned to Young Woman and gave her a look at once casually companionable and also meant to convey the heavy import of what she had once shared with me. A look that said, *Alone at last. I never told anyone, you know. That thing we share. Remember?*

But she didn't seem to. Her eyes lingered over my face in the most fleeting and casual manner before she went back to cracking the wafer of ice on a puddle with the toe of her boot. Hearing Yuval turning the dead bolt on the church door, she brushed past me, muttering, "Well, *this* was a fucking waste of time," as she headed for the car.

There would be many more instances like this, where the people who had told me things had no memory of it, or at least claimed not to. Perhaps one day I will have heard too much. I will be a living reminder of someone else's shame and be dropped as a result. It hasn't really happened yet. For the most part, we all go on. With luck, the canker of the most terrible secret eventually stops throbbing, although there's really no predicting how someone will weather having spilled their beans, just that they will spill them. That is inevitable. We are disclosing animals, wired for unburdening. It's what we do as a species. When I am being told, I listen, mindful of the honor, remembering all the while that the shore would be mistaken to believe that the waves lap up against him because he is so beautiful.

A Capacity for Wonder

Three Expeditions

Her tone was rhetorical, only half amused and sawtoothed with mild irritation.

"Do you like *anything*?" she asked me.

I'd heard it, or words to this effect, many times before. A reductive verdict that paints me as impervious to joy. I am not. What I am is the opposite of an adrenaline junkie, essentially allergic to the hormone. I once spent close to a week paddling like a madman over Class V rapids while whitewater rafting through Chilean Patagonia with Robert F. Kennedy Junior. I am not speaking metaphorically here, how I wish I were. I really *did* whitewater raft through Chilean Patagonia with RFK Jr. and family. It suffices to say that a nicer, smarter, nobler man you could never hope to meet, but it was an excursion and activity I would only ever repeat at high-gauge, hollow-tip-bullet-loaded gunpoint. Those five days unleashed a largely continuous endocrine cascade that flooded my brain with the stressor and just made me feel weak and jittery, whereas it seemed only to make everyone else's eyes bluer, their bone structure more patrician and to just generally quicken and galvanize the life force coursing through their healthy Christian bloodstreams.

And so what if it is also true that I am incapable, when entering a beautiful old movie palace, for instance, to simply gaze in wonder at its gilded rococo froth without also simultaneously scanning the room for the comforting red lettering of the nearest fire exit. Or, when traveling by subway (front car, always) between Manhattan and Brooklyn, I read my newspaper while remaining conscious at all times of the subtle shift in incline, the slight pop in the ears that indicates the halfway point under the river, which will prove useful in determining whether I would swim forward to the next station or back whence we came in the unlikely event the tunnel filled with water. That doesn't make me immune to pleasure.

"I like everything," I replied, feeling misrepresented and only half amused right back. "I don't hate the world. I'm scared of it. There's a difference." I wanted to tell her that she was only getting half the story. But if one is staying in and saying "I'd rather not," whether the disinclination is born of anhedonia or of fear, the distinction is academic at best.

And so it came to pass, in a moment of dark recrimination, sick and tired of these Bartleby tendencies, and in want of a healthy dose of alacrity, hopefulness, and appetite, I lit out for the territories—a counterphobic campaign to see the handiwork of the men and women who said Yes. My destinations: one striving for perfection upon this earth; one a monument to undying love from friends and strangers alike; and one a mere way station to a heavenly reward. Constructed Edens, all three.

I.

Great Expectations

Tom Morrow is naked but for his clear plastic lab coat, although the peekaboo effect only reveals a sexless Lucite-over-circuitry body, supporting an Arcimboldo face of transistors beneath a stiff brush cut of copper hair. It is Tom Morrow we must glide by, Tom Morrow we must heed before we can reach our destination. As voiced by Nathan Lane, Tom Morrow is a schticky Cerberus guarding the gates of the Future, waggling his titanium eyebrows, singing a show tune about the great, big, beautiful tomorrow that awaits us all, a suburban paradise of unconditional leisure where our lawns will be mowed robotically. Tom Morrow promises us techno-wonders the likes of which we have never seen before: "And I'm not talking about Mr. Coffee, whose work I admire," he jokes. A gag that invokes a device none of the younger folks in the crowd will remember should have been the first sign, but before we have time to register the fact, the moving floor has carried us along and we have been deposited at the front door of the Disney Innoventions Dream Home.

Clad in fieldstone set with arts-and-crafts wooden doors with Tiffany-style glass transoms, overhung with lattice hung with artificial flowers, it looks like a high-end casino. In the art nouveau ironwork of the railings one can make out that unmistakable circle, topped at ten and two o'clock by two smaller circles—the silhouette of the Mouse That Started It All. This bit of slipped-in iconography is known within Disneyland as a Hidden Mickey. It's an actual Term of Art around here and one can spend hours trying to suss them out throughout the park, like looking for the "Ninas" in Hirschfeld drawings.

An interest in speculative social engineering has always been a part of the Disney mission. Epcot, now by all accounts little more than a glorified food court, stands for Experimental Prototype Community of Tomorrow. The Dream Home follows in the steps of Tomorrowland's original utopian domicile, the Monsanto House of the Future, sponsored by that corporation's division of plastics, before the very word became an ironic joke. Opened in 1957, it was meant to represent a home in 1986. The Monsanto House featured such theretofore unheard-of marvels as a microwave, an ultrasonic dishwasher that rose from beneath the counter, closed-circuit-TV intercoms, and an electric razor. Old footage shows that it really was a wonder. A gorgeous building with walls of plastic windows, perched atop a central post, echoing Buckminster Fuller's visionary Dymaxion House. The House of the Future was simultaneously sleek and voluptuous; imagine a gigantic futuristic cold-water faucet: a lovely white plus sign of a building with the mid-century grace of Eero Saarinen's TWA terminal, gently inflated like a water wing.

Contemporary accounts of the advent of electricity on the domestic front almost always make mention of a horrified realization of the kinds of filth people lived with before they could see it properly illuminated. The House of the Future's atomic-age promise was a similar serenity born of cleanliness and the ease of achieving same. Built in an America of widespread prosperity, the brief efflorescence of sexual equality during World War II having been effectively quashed, it was a house that would be kept not by a promised slave class of robots doing all the work, as in Tom Morrow's song, but by a growing middle class of servantless women. Economically scaled and compact—the boy's and girl's rooms were separated by a retractable wall—it was the extreme convenience of surfaces that could be wiped down, clutter that could be concealed behind immaculate laminate panels, that figures so heavily in the narration ("Here's the answer to the continuous activity of the younger set . . . tough, durable, easily washable . . . Plastic, in combination with plywood, fiberglass . . . even the fabrics on the furniture are of man-made fibers," says the voice-over. And then the proud kicker, "*hardly a natural material appears anywhere*"). The House of the Future stood near the entrance to Tomorrowland for a decade, until 1967. Apparently, the wrecking ball simply bounced off and the structure had to be taken apart piece by piece and carted away.

The Innoventions Dream Home is not a freestanding dwelling like its predecessor. It's not even a full home. There is neither a master bedroom nor a bathroom. Instead it is a series of representative rooms occupying the ground floor of the Innoventions building, a two-story structure built in 1967 to house the General Electric Carousel of Progress. Innoventions was opened in 1998 as a hands-on, interactive exhibit that showcased the latest technological devices, such as voice-activated computers, high-definition TVs, and smart-cars. The second floor still has a driving course with a freaky psychedelic backdrop of planets and spaceships where one can try out a Segway, the device that was supposed to change everything but instead ended up as a punch line.

While we're on the subject of outsized claims that border on the risible, can we pause for a moment to talk about that term, Innovention? A neologism that, in an effort to turbo-charge meaning, takes two perfectly eloquent and unassailable words and by combining them renders both suspect. It is a word developed by committee, one that can only be spoken unironically if one is being paid to do so, like menus in chain restaurants that list "Snacketizers" and "Appeteasers." Can't you just taste the process-mapping? The neon-orange layer of melted reconstituted-milk-solids-derived "cheese," the pink stratum of animal-protein-cultured "meat"? Vacuum-packed and irradiated and shipped to some franchise that itself was unpacked from boxes sent directly from corporate, with ready-made walls of homey, weathered fake brick and battered retro license plates. "Innovention" can only leave a similar taste in the mouth. It makes one suspicious, wondering about the ways in which the object in question is found so wanting, so insufficiently innovative or lacking in invention to warrant this linguistic boost.

The home is a partnership between the theme park, a housing developer called Taylor Morrison, and various software companies, including Microsoft. Disney hired a playwright, Greg Atkins, and an art director, Tom Zofrea, in order to raise a visit to the Dream Home over and above mere electronics-showroom gawking, to create an "immersive" experience, an environment peopled by actual characters with an actual story. So the Dream Home is where the Elias family lives (another sort of Hidden Mickey, Elias was Walt Disney's middle name). There is no formal script to speak of so much as a governing narrative, which is as follows: young Robbie Elias, age ten, scored the final goal for his soccer team, the Astro Blasters, thereby winning them the championship. The entire Elias family is off to Beijing for the finals and they're having a big bash to celebrate and we, complete strangers, are invited.

There are multiple actors filling each role. The casting hews closely to the TV sitcom model, where the dads are fat guys reassuringly married to hot moms. There is a soccer coach, a supportive next-door neighbor (as well as her nosy counterpart, played by the same person, as best as I can tell from the show's "bible" with which I am provided), a teenage daughter, and two grandparents to round out the characters: Grandma's feisty and Grandpa is a good-natured fumferer. Both are shockingly young-looking.

The saga begins with Brian Elias, the dad, an architect, stepping out of the front door in his yellow soccer jersey and welcoming us, *Our Town*–like, with a monologue. "Hey everybody, how you doin'? You're all here for the party. Well, as you probably know, my son Robbie's soccer team, the Astro Blasters, just won the national championship and we are headed to China for the finals. Yeah!!! Not to brag too much but Robbie did score the winning goal. It was so cool. It was even covered by *Good Morn-*

ing America. We recorded it. It's playing in the family room. Check it out. We all ready to party? Let's go in!"

But wait! Things suddenly take a decidedly Ibsen turn. For you see, Brian Elias is locked out. Of his very own home. O, bitter irony for this architect by trade, this master builder, if you will. No worry, he shows us a fob that can open the door electronically. But "I'm really prone to losing things," he tells us. "Like keys, fobs, *my mind during tax time.*" So he can also make use of the hand scanner that reads his palm as he passes it over an electronic console. Suddenly the Tiffany transoms fade away and are replaced by the telltale contrail of Tinker Bell tracing her phosphorescent path across the entire façade of his home. Brian runs through changing the windows to holiday displays for Halloween, the Fourth of July, and Christmas. "I'll never have to untangle a string of lights again," he tells us with a satisfied chuckle.

I am on a walk-through with Greg Atkins, the playwright. Aesthetically, the Dream Home is a mix of styles, a warm place full of wood, earth tones, and a multitude of well-chosen knick-knacks (all nailed down, not surprisingly). There are none of the Jetsonian fins and boomerangs nor surgical whites of an Apple Store that one associates with a past or present-day cutting-edge environment. The future, such as it is, is behind the walls, most notably in something called the Life/ware system, which has touch pads at the entrance to each room. Icons on the screen correspond to each Elias family member. When Dad presses his button, for example, the room adjusts itself to his various pre-programmed preferences: lighting, shades up or shades down, music playing, even the images that are displayed in the many digital picture frames all around. For Brian, who is an architect, the photos switch to things structural: an ink drawing of the

Leaning Tower of Pisa, a view of London with Norman Foster's Gherkin office tower visible, as well as the double-helix ramps in his dome for the Reichstag in Berlin.

Atkins is an incredibly friendly guy who, while having enjoyed the experience of working on the Dream Home, hardly seems like a Kool-Aid drinker. He is pleased when I can identify a wall mural as being in the style of Maxfield Parrish, and downright thrilled when we enter the home for the first time and he has us turn left, because most people turn right, and I say "Paco Underwood," referring to the retail anthropologist who observed this phenomenon (something I only know from reading Malcolm Gladwell). Either way, it earns me major points, which I proceed to lose five minutes later.

Above the door to the kitchen, a cross-stitch sampler reads KEEP IT SIMPLE. If spare means simple, then this spa-like kitchen is the place. The backsplashes are thick plastic embedded with yellow gingko leaves; a kidney-bean-shaped central island is of some icy frosted polymer. Even the sink is confoundingly austere, nothing more than a round stainless basin and a small metal lever. "Press down on it," Atkins tells me. I do, and the faucet rises from underneath the counter like a curious asp. It is incredibly cool, and being able to retract something that might chip a plate or interfere with washing vegetables seems a genuinely practical application. Not so much the voice-activated kitchen computer. Like all omniscient machines possessed of benevolent intent but lacking decision-making power, it is a she. "Lillian" (Lillian was the name of Mrs. Disney) can read the radio frequency identification tag on a bag of flour, for example, and suggest recipes. She knows when one has run out of an ingredient and can connect to an online grocer and order more. That seems convenient enough, but does it require that one affix these RFID tags to all of one's ingredients so that they fall within

Lillian's purview? That seems like a lot more work than writing a shopping list. More likely such items will be purchased already tagged by the supermarket. But will Lillian know, for example, when I'm down to three cloves of garlic? Enough for a sauce but a woefully short supply if I were contemplating making a gazpacho (he worried faggily).

I try some of the cupboards, which do not open. I think that, like on many stage sets, these are false fronts, until it is pointed out that we have punched the Dad preferences on the console. Apparently Dad engages with the kitchen on a strictly need-to-know basis, which instantly brings up associations to clandestine contents in drawers, Betty Friedan's "the problem that has no name," and the Rolling Stones song "Mother's Little Helper." Does pressing "Mom" give me an all-access pass to the bottle of Valium? The cabinet that holds the "personal massager" or box of cornstarch with the secret diaphragm in it, which is taken out and used during the joyless afternoon countertop rutting with Pedro, the grocery delivery boy ('scuse us, Lillian)? Oh, Eliases, what darkness you all conceal.

The picture frames on the breakfast-room walls show shifting images of children's artwork. Authentic examples of "Best Dad in the World" type drawings made by Atkins's own children, he tells me. This is Ignored Hint Number One. There are also beautiful food-related photographs of a coffee cup in Paris, bins of brightly colored spices at outdoor markets, all taken by Atkins from his travels. Ignored Hint Number Two: he is *all over* this room. Taking a fridge magnet printed with a bakery logo from a drawer, Atkins goes to the interactive "bulletin board," and rubs the magnet against its surface. A lovely little girl comes up on the screen. Her name is Cassidy and she greets us and invites us to order baked goods. "Do you think that's a pretty girl?" he asks me.

Suppose you are at a party. A man comes up to you, holding a silver tray of canapés. On his starched white shirtfront, there is a gaping, bleeding hole, the exact shape and size of his heart, revealing a glistening, bloody void. When you look down to his tray, what you see arrayed on all the toast points are slices of red flesh. You spy a valve, and something that looks very much like a section of aorta. Moreover, all the hors d'oeuvres are still pulsing with the life that only recently coursed through them. So when the man asks you if you would like to try one, and then adds, his voice laden with import, "I made them for you myself," do you upend his tray, sending the snacks flying with a dismissive and disgusted, "Fuck no! That looks like heart and I loathe heart and anyone stupid enough to serve it to me!" Do you say that? No, you do not.

Unless you are an idiot.

So. "Do you think that's a pretty girl?" he asks.

Because I am in Disneyland, where the dewiest nymphs seem more often than not the farthest thing from innocent, with a habit of disrobing for Annie Leibovitz or bearing children at the advanced age of sixteen, I allow as how yes, she seems lovely, if not a mite "chillingly professional."

She is Tom Atkins's daughter.

Atkins is too nice and classy a guy to do anything but laugh at my faux pas, but I beat a hasty retreat to the bedroom of the fictional teenage daughter (I read somewhere that she is named Chelsea, but the poor thing needs to work on her self-esteem since she introduces herself with a "Hi, I'm the daughter"). Two of the walls are interactive bulletin boards that can show artwork, photos, and movies. But the main attraction is her Magic Mirror. Looking through the glass at a camera, I am body-mapped and my face is scanned and refracted into an Eiffel Tower fretwork of planes and angles. The computer now recognizes me and, like the daughter, I can try on outfits virtually, without the tedium of having to actually disrobe and reclothe myself. The mirror offers me choices of hairstyles, accessories, dresses, etc. As a test, I am given a luxurian 'do of cascading black hair. Looking into the mirror, which has the tiniest time delay, the "hair" superimposes itself around my head, ebony and shiny and immovable as lacquered beetle wings. The dress they put on my body is a CGI creation, as smooth and undifferentiated as the skin of a dolphin. I am a bosomy porpoise. The garment, meant to simulate a swaying skirt, undulates like a sea anemone, even though I am not moving.

The son, Robbie Elias, has a bed shaped like a pirate ship in his bedroom. By opening a chip-enabled copy of *Peter Pan*, something as simple as story time can be turned into a wholly different animal. The room is transformed into a sound-and-light show, with clips from the animated classic, full orchestral music, and Tinker Bell zooming past the windows and setting lampshades to spinning and drawers to slamming. At one point, the cannon at the foot of the bed begins to smoke, signaling its readiness to fire. Pulling the rope at the end of the barrel somehow causes it to shoot invisible cannonballs that pierce holes in the pillowy banks of clouds on the movie screens on the opposite walls. It's very cool, but very, very stimulating. (Goodnight bowl of mush, Goodnight . . . *oncoming speeding locomotive train!*) An ancient and unimpeachably wholesome act of parenting is reengineered to be the equivalent of hooking one's kid up to a glucose drip five minutes before bedtime. It also relieves any child of the task of using his imagination. The same thing happens in the dining room, where Atkins takes out an Eiffel Tower snow globe from a bibelot cabinet. Placing it on a special lighted shelf, the frames around us change to pictures from the Elias family vacation to France. "Then we can talk about our trip," he says. *Or,* I think, *we could talk about our trip. Someone has only to say, "Hey, remember that awesome trip we took to France?"*

The Dream Home is, at best, an upgrade of gadgets already familiar to most people, like photo albums, for example. That kitchen faucet is undeniably nifty, and a coffee table whose surface is an interactive screen where one can page through a virtual copy of the original manuscript of Lewis Carroll's *Alice's Adventures Under Ground,* downloaded from the British Library (a large iPad, basically, but we don't know that yet), is absolutely covet-worthy. There is even some mild amusement in the Magic Mirror. But what might have been truly new, exciting, or groundbreaking has been punted on (more of that in a moment), leaving Atkins and Zofrea to sex up what is ultimately an electronics showroom for crowds, most of whom are carrying telephones that can already do half of the stuff here.

Does the Elias Family Saga turn this trade show into an immersive experience? One is certainly deposited into a sea of people. They let in groups of seventy visitors at a time, but guests can stay as long as they like and the space fills up in very short order. Another impediment is that the Elias characters never interact with one another—kind of a basic requirement for a dramatic entertainment—so the carefully constructed back-stories and relationships might as well never have been written in the first place. Moreover, they're all wearing the same yellow Astro Blasters jersey, which makes them seem like less dramatis personae than employees at a Best Buy. And no one, neither guest nor Elias, is sticking around long enough to have anything but the most glancing contact. They appear, greet us, say something breathless and generic about their upcoming trip to China while directing our attention to some gadget, and then beat a hasty retreat with a cheerful "See you at the party out back. Have fun!" To cut them some slack, there is almost no way to inject emotional urgency into the phrase "See, my iPac phone connects with the Life/ware system that connects through Microsoft Windows . . ."—but why even try? The narrative hook of the Elias family and their "story" is about as effective as decorating bullets. Who's going to appreciate the flowers that have been lovingly painted on as they whiz by?

Actually, a bullet—decorated or unadorned—starts to look mighty attractive after a while once the crowds come in. The Dream Home is a place of ceaseless activity and cacophony. The Life/ware consoles compete with one another from room to room. The light levels cycle rapidly. The window shades—printed in an attractive Alphonse Mucha–style swirl—rise and fall like carousel horses. The crowds want to try things out, pitting Dad's Barry White against Mom's ABBA not twenty feet away. At one point I park myself near one of the control panels and unilaterally select Grandpa's Andrews Sisters playlist, not giving anyone who approaches even the slimmest of chances of changing the music for a few blessed minutes. This is just one of the many dispiriting aspects of 360 Tomorrowland Way: it would be just as jangling even without visitors, if it was only the family here. Rooms reassemble themselves upon the arrival of a new Elias, responding to RFID tags sewn into their soccer jerseys (although if two people enter the room at the same time, Mom's preferences prevail, the Peace of the Hearth being of paramount importance). Things chez Elias are both adversarial and negligent, as though a family with shared interests who might agree upon what to hang on the walls of the dining room was somewhat laughable, as though we have all of us, up until now, been living lives of quiet desperation, muffling our desires and personal preferences in ambient music, lighting, cuisine, and artwork. The Life/ware system is predicated on the notion that the personal preferences of each family member are inimically different. And such environment-shifting software seems a questionable power to bestow upon a child, if only because of its potential narrowing of horizons. The notion of guiding a juvenile mind away from a constant diet of *The Suite Life of Zack and Cody* might seem heretical here at Disney, but surely shaping the tastes of the young is a fundamental part of taking care of them, a more benign aspect of the moral attentiveness that makes us inoculate them against disease and teach them not to steal. Is the fear of a tantrum so great that a Brueghel painting, say, must perforce morph into a large photo of a gumball machine just because an eight-year-old has walked into the room?

Passing the Parrish-style mural on the courtyard wall—beside the very ordinary laundry room that still filled this apartment dweller with envious wonder—I head to the much talked-about party out back, in the AstroTurfed "yard." With an expected eight thousand visitors marching through the space every day, any natural grass would be trampled into oblivion just as surely as if it had been napalmed. It resembles a car commercial set in a dealership where there is a balloon-festooned shindig in progress. Will we all kiss at midnight? Unlikely, since there isn't a scrap of sustenance or drop of inhibition-lowering liquid in sight. With a cocktail or two, this could become the scene in DeMille's *The Ten Commandments* where the Israelites, doubting the existence of their god, smelt a golden calf to worship—and for some nubile contract players to writhe upon—the bacchanal reaching its acme just as Moses returns with the tablets of the Law in hand, and you know the rest of *that* story . . .

A major aspect of the party that is preventing the kind of unenlightened behavior that goeth before a fall is the fact that no one is looking at anyone else. There is a deafening chaos of competing Zunes (Microsoft's MP3 players), a Taylor Morrison Homes design-it-yourself monitor, a race-car simulation game complete with juddering driver's seat (what garden would be complete without one?), and a barbecue with a flat-screen monitor that can dispense cooking instructions, but no food. And there, a vanquished Apollo, now reduced to serving as nothing but a decorative pedestal for another noise-dispensing screen, is a small-scale model of the original House of the Future.

It is a dog pile of consumption, overhung with colored Chinese lanterns. It all makes one yearn for the monastic serenity of the Times Square subway at rush hour. The cherry on this sundae of despair is the helium squeak of two little girls karaoke-ing their way through the main anthem from *High School Musical,* the *musica sacra* of the tween canon, "Start of Something New." Frankly, it all feels anything but.

At five thousand square feet, the Dream Home is plush and commodious. In the entire place, the only thing that might qualify as a space-saving Innovention is that kitchen faucet. Otherwise, nothing is dual-purpose; nothing folds down into anything else. Nowhere is there even a tip of the hat to a world of dwindling resources or our dependence on fossil fuels, foreign or domestic. Far more than the atomic-age louvers and aerodynamic icing of the fifty-year-old versions of the future, this house seems mired in yesterday. Your grandfather's tomorrow was more ingenious. Atkins doesn't really understand my reservations, thinking that my problems with the Dream Home are aesthetic. "We're in Southern California. We think *this* way," spreading his hands wide apart, "not *this* way," he says, spacing them vertically. Precisely.

Art director Tom Zofrea gets it. He acknowledges and applauds the current trends toward mixed-use, human-scale homes and neighborhoods, with the lost art of walking enjoying a locomotive renaissance. "If you read the architectural literature and what architects are looking at for the future, they are looking at reinventing the mixed-use, New York flats above the retail space. I actually think that's a great way to go, it sends the right message, absolutely positive." Why then does this have no place in the Dream Home? The reasons are both practical and philosophical. With Americans with Disabilities Act accessibility requirements and fire-code compliances, there would be almost no way to make it much more compact. True enough, but the conspicuous absence of even a mention of alternative fuel sources, of solar or wind power, smacks of marching orders from on high. "What we're trying to do is to keep a very optimistic and open view of the future, and the optimistic view of the future is 'we'll solve these problems and we'll learn to design around them,'" he says. The Dream Home, therefore, exists in an unspecified time and space when the challenges of oil and sprawl have been vanquished, although how exactly is never mentioned. Disney may have said it first but they seem to have forgotten that it really is a small world, after all.

In an odd coincidence, the very week that the Dream Home opened, at the other end of the Disney corporation's spectrum, Pixar releases *Wall-E,* its thoroughly dystopian masterpiece, a film premised on a world choked by garbage and waste, a planet no longer habitable and made so, at least in part, by—let's not mince words—the fat fucks who build gargantuan homes that make little or no concession to the limited resources out there.

The Monsanto House of the Future actually began as a research project between the chemical company and MIT as a means of exploring the ways in which plastics and man-made materials could be harnessed in ways they never had been previously. The original promotional film begins by speaking rapturously of the many wondrous innovations (see how lovely a word that is, all on its own?) that had already vastly improved lives: waterproof roofing materials; shockproof vinyl coverings for electrical cords; materials that could be produced industrially and cheaply. "This is indeed a revolution," says the voice-over.

The current revolution—one that Disney has ignored here—is sustainability. We should be walking through a five-hundred-square-foot home where you cook with, drink, urinate, heat, cool, and drink once more the same four gallons of water. The overwhelming feeling here is of a home from 2004, already ancient history in the public consciousness, pre–subprime mortgage crisis and the collapse of the world economy. The paint is barely dry and this is already out-of-date; a timid, delusional, exurban mausoleum that can only be accessed by a decreasingly affordable car (the Monsanto House didn't even have a garage). More than the waste, the equating of acknowledging reality with bumming people out is what seems most glaringly old school. By the time I visit in late 2008, we are already shuddering on the brink of a cultural moment where, after suffering through years of falsely elevated and baseless hopes, it feels downright animated-woodland-creature-chirpy to face up to facts. A young fellow waiting to get into the Dream Home wears a T-shirt whose sentiments presage the necessary tough times ahead which still hold the promise of the rosiest of new dawns: 1-20-09. BUSH'S LAST DAY.

It's not a total bust. The Dream Home does provide one moment of absolutely authentic wish fulfillment: a father in the family room, in front of the vast, gorgeous, pool-table-sized sheet of glass that is the Elias family television set. He is on the sofa, asleep.

II.
The Boulevard of Broken Dreams

Superman has taken the morning off. Although appearing among us in mufti, he is immediately identifiable by his square jaw and the comma of dark hair upon his forehead. With an affable hello he greets the other Hollywood Boulevard regulars who have gathered along with a small crowd of tourists standing outside the classical façade of the old Masonic Temple, now the theater where Jimmy Kimmel does his evening talk show. The USC Trojans marching band, or at least a skeleton crew thereof, goes through its paces, a casually synchronized, loose-limbed routine in which they instrumentally exhort us to do a little dance, make a little love, and above all, get down tonight. Superman bops his head, enjoying his moments of freedom. In a while he will have to put on his blue tights and red Speedo and go in to work, posing for pictures with the tourists in front of Grauman's Chinese Theatre. Maybe he'll stop on the way at the Coffee Bean & Tea Leaf at the corner of Hollywood and North Orange. Batman and the Cat in the Hat go there sometimes.

Suddenly, from the doors of the theater, just behind the Trojans, emerges a cheerful chubby fellow. Completely unconnected to the proceedings on the street, he is dressed in a cheap red-satin Satan costume. Dancing in time to the music, he beckons to us, crowing delightedly, "Worship *me*! Worship *me*!"

But we are here for neither the Man of Steel nor the Prince of Darkness. We have come this morning to witness the consecration of the newest star on Hollywood's Walk of Fame. The "star" in question on this dull April morning is local radio personality Dan Avey, who will join the two thousand–plus others—from the greats to the somewhat less-than-greats to the downright obscure—in that characteristic luncheon-meat-pink-against-lustrous-black-terrazzo-and-brass immortality. The Hollywood Chamber of Commerce, the organization that administers the Walk, has set up a steel barrier to separate those with a personal stake in the ceremony from the gawkers and hoi polloi. It is a hopeful gesture.

"It's almost like going to your own funeral," says Avey, after the brief tributes from fellow radio announcers. The star is unveiled. Avey's friends and family applaud. A local crazy snaps pictures; his straw fedora is banded with a braid of blue-and-white balloons, the kind birthday-party clowns twist into animal and flower shapes, and his ears sport very large fake diamonds. He is trying to get a knot of puzzled German tourists to move, but he squeaks out a high-pitched gibberish that only seems to increase his frustration, as the Germans just look at him. Perplexed Northern Europeans—hereafter PNEs—turn out to be just one of the mainstays of the area, along with leafleting evangelicals, sex workers, harmless ambulant schizophrenics, and beat cops.

There are some places where an intrinsic melancholy might be reason enough to stay away, I suppose, although I can't think of any. Hollywood Boulevard recently underwent a major urban renewal, a charge led by the building of the Kodak Theatre complex, current home of the Oscars and *American Idol* telecasts. But the neighborhood's dilapidated, honky-tonk charms, and they are legion, lie in the vestiges of its storied past that endure obstinately: Grauman's Egyptian Theatre, currently home of the American Cinematheque, with its sandstone forecourt and hieroglyphics, looking like something straight out of the Valley of the Kings; the polychrome-plaster opulence of the El Capitan Theatre, restored and now owned by Disney; the affronted but intact dignity of Marlene Dietrich's star as it sits for eternity in front of Greco's New York Pizzeria; similarly the star of June Havoc, baby sister to Gypsy Rose Lee, which welcomes shoppers to the rubber and fetish extravaganza of Pleasure's Treasures. Only a heartless ogre would fail to be touched by a protective affection for Hollywood Boulevard. It is trying its best. Hollywood Boulevard makes you want to take care of it.

It was ever thus, it seems. Gleaming new theme restaurants and chain stores fail to get at what has always been the essence of the neighborhood. Like other cultural institutions whose heyday is perpetually a thing of the past—reports of the death of the Broadway musical that have been around as long as the musicals themselves come to mind—Hollywood Boulevard was born a little bit sad. The Walk of Fame, for example, was conceived as a means of sprucing up the neighborhood as far back as 1960 when they, ahem, laid Joanne Woodward. Even farther back the writer Nathaneal West lived in a hotel on the boulevard and set his 1939 novel, *The Day of the Locust,* in and around its environs. West's dark tale of Hollywood concludes gruesomely with two senseless murders and a frenzied crowd out of control, whipped into a fervor of lawlessness by the sweeping klieg lights and bottlenecking barricades of a movie premiere at Kahn's Persian Palace Theatre, a thinly veiled reference to Sid Grauman's Chinese Theatre.

Things are a good deal tamer on the day I visit, as tourists mill about the theater's courtyard, posing with costumed characters—for the most part fictional superheroes, with the exception of a late-Vegas-vintage Elvis—and looking over the hand- and footprints of Hollywood immortals. The tradition was supposedly begun when silent-film star Norma Talmadge was walking in front of the theater and inadvertently stepped into some wet cement. The most popular square remains the joint one of Marilyn Monroe and Jane Russell, a title presumably conferred by the number of people posing in front of it. No one is standing by the *Gentlemen Prefer Blondes* co-stars this morning, although a young African American woman has her picture taken with her hands nestled into the prints of Denzel Washington. Elsewhere, a five-year-old Scandinavian boy (cf. earlier reference to PNEs) dutifully places his tiny mitts into the depressions made by Depression-era cutie-pie Joan Blondell. You know how Swedish kindergartners go mad for *Gold Diggers of 1933.*

Grauman's Chinese is one of the loveliest and most impressive buildings it has ever been my privilege to enter, with beautifully marked fire exits, to boot. If you go to Los Angeles and do not see it, then you are a dope, as I was the first dozen times I visited that town. It must be an oversight most people make, because there are only four of us on the tour. Where most opulent movie palaces are great, neo-Versailles meringues, Grauman's Chinese is a lavish exercise in Orientalist escape. The murals that adorn the walls and ceilings of the place, skillful and beautiful traditional Chinese ornamental scenes, were done by Guangzhou-born actor Keye Luke, most famous as Number One Son of non-Chinese actor Warner Oland in the Charlie Chan films.

More movie premieres are held in Grauman's than in any other theater, ever since 1927, when it hosted its first, Cecil B. DeMille's *The King of Kings.* The prime seats in the theater are rows seven, eight, and nine, reserved for whosoever is starring in that night's film. Indicating a seat in this hallowed section, our tour guide says, "Ray Romano sat here for *Ice Age.*" Then, so as to assure us that all the seats are good ones, he points to the front of the house and says, "For the premiere of *Along Came Polly,* John Travolta and his lovely wife, Kelly Preston, sat down there."

Our guide. Sigh. In his cheap tuxedo at midday, with his mild manner, weak chin, and a face scarified by the ravages of adolescence, he is the embodiment of a doomed and guileless purity, the hapless pawn set upon by the townspeople in a misguided riot of mob mentality. Or perhaps I've got Nathaneal West on the brain. But our docent does seem like the classic victim. Even his evident love for the theater is given short shrift by the powers that be, because throughout the tour, the Grauman's sound system vomits out a meaningless and distractingly loud montage of partial commercials, snippets of songs, and bits of movie trailers.

We are led outside and up the outdoor escalator of the theater complex/mini-mall, to the adjoining Mann Chinese 6 Theatre. We are being given a tour of a multiplex built in 2001. My underpants are older than the Mann 6. A greasy usher opens the door for us on the second floor. "Welcome to the VIP area," he leers. (Okay, he's not that greasy and not really leering, but there is such a sideshow shadiness to the "value added" aspect of this leg of the tour and, let me reiterate, we don't need to be here! Grauman's by itself is sublime and sufficient!) The VIP area is neither all that "V" nor "I." It is just a loungy part of the theater where, for an extra twenty dollars, you can sit and order concessions and they'll be delivered to your seat. Or you can play chess or checkers or read a book, our guide tells us, pointing to a wall where there isn't a book in sight. "Go ahead and sit in one of the chairs so you can feel what it's like," says our guide. We all remain standing.

The tour ends, as such things do, in the gift shop, where we see two old projectors from Grauman's, which are kind of cool, and also two wax figures of Chinese coolies that once stood in the theater lobby. Rubbing them used to be considered good luck. Our guide then lets us in on a secret. "There are many people who come to the theater and see how authentic it is and are then under the mistaken impression that Sid Grauman was himself Chinese. He wasn't," he says, disabusing us of an apparently oft-held Hollywood myth. "He was Irish and Jewish." *Who,* I think, *are the genius demographers who think someone named Sid Grauman was Chinese?* But my unspoken outrage is drowned out by "Sugar Pie, Honey Bunch," which blasts over the gift-shop sound system throughout his talk.

A little spent, I return to my hotel. Luckily, I am staying right across the street at the beautiful Hollywood Roosevelt, a lovely building erected in 1927. A cool, dark, Spanish-colonial folly of a place with a central lobby that has a tile floor and a splashing fountain, it's like Norma Desmond's house in *Sunset Boulevard* if she started taking in guests. The similarities don't stop at the architecture, actually. There are moments where it distinctly feels like things are being run by a delusional Gloria Swanson. The frustrations are minute but widespread: the wooden ledge that runs the length of my room and doubles as my headboard is gray with dust and remains so throughout my stay. Every time I ask reception to call me a cab, I am told affable words to the effect of "Right away"; my request is then radioed out to one of the attendants in the driveway not twenty feet distant, indicating my imminent arrival out the door in, oh, about five seconds, along with a description of what I am wearing. I emerge from the hotel into a scrum of attendants with headsets and whistles, ready to be of service, and I am invisible. This happens over and over again. The sense one gets at the Roosevelt is that they have bigger fish to fry. Or cuter and younger fish, at any rate. The very first Academy Awards ceremony was held at the Roosevelt in 1929 and the hotel is once more at the burning center of movie-star currency. Young women in skinny jeans and stilettos, accompanied by their men in untucked striped oxford shirts and premium denim, flock each night to the Roosevelt's bar, a hopping establishment called Teddy's that, just prior to my arrival, had been embroiled in a minor scandal when the impresaria, "nightlife producer" Amanda Scheer Demme, was dismissed, ostensibly for allowing (I am shocked, *shocked!*) underage drinking by young celebrities. There were further accusations against

Demme that she had made the actual guests of the hotel feel unwelcome at Teddy's (again, permit my organs to rupture in surprise). Actually, I wouldn't know since I cannot find the place no matter how many hallways I try. I can hear the thumping of the sound system each day starting at dusk. I enter many a disused ballroom thinking that this must be the way, but I still cannot tell you where it is. Does the Roosevelt have a gym? I have no idea. I do know there is a pool, apparently painted by David Hockney. I've seen pictures in magazines, and it's quite pretty, plus the juxtapositional joke of Hockney applying paint *to* the very object he's famous for rendering *in* paint is amusing, but again, no sign in the elevator telling me where it might be and staff members who can seem downright yeti-like in their elusiveness.

The exclusion I feel at the Roosevelt is not unlike living in the apartment directly beneath Valhalla, a feeling only amplified one morning when I go across the street to the Coffee Bean & Tea Leaf to see Thor standing outside holding a latte. His helmet is a plastic rendition of beaten metal and animal horns, with a fall of synthetic flaxen hair sewn onto the inside edge. The locks spill down over his "bare" shoulders, in reality the sleeves of his costume, a shiny flesh-colored fabric. The musculature is sewn directly into the garment, meant to mimic the bulging biceps and ropey forearms of the Norse god of war. But the stitches around the pillowy inserts are visible, and the whole thing bags and wrinkles around his skinny arms. "You guys drinking later?" he asks his friends, his mouth a checkerboard of intact and missing teeth.

He could use the kind of makeover once promised in the Johnny Mercer song (". . . *if you think that you can be an actor, see Mister Factor, He'd make a monkey look good. Within a half an hour, You'll look like Tyrone Power, Hooray for Hollywood!*), and he'd be in luck, because the original Max Factor makeup studio is just down the street. A perfect pink deco boîte of a building, picked out here and there with golden-plaster detailing of fabric swags, it is terribly chic and female and locks like an enormous jewel box from a Busby Berkeley number, whose lid might at any moment open to reveal five hundred pairs of legs dancing on a mirror-finish floor. To look around it is to smell pressed powder and Final Net with your eyes. The ancient woman who methodically takes my money and hands me back my change with a painstaking if glacial precision is still sporting a hairstyle straight out of *Swing Time*. She might well have been one of the marcelled beauties who paraded these halls back when it was still a salon. It has since been turned into the Hollywood History Museum, the ground floor concerning Max Factor's specific role in the dream factory. A series of small rooms is devoted, respectively, to a different hair color and that shade's most iconic star. The For Blondes Only room claims Lana Turner and Marilyn Monroe, among others. Brunettes boasts Liz Taylor as its figurehead. The For Redheads Only room loves Lucy, naturally. And then I come upon a room reserved for "Brownettes," which is a new one on me and sounds like the affectionate name one might give a much loved and highly effective barbiturate. How fitting, then, that the Brownette for the ages is none other than Judy Garland.

I keep up the period perfection and take lunch at Musso and Frank, a little farther east. Opened in 1919, the restaurant makes an appearance in *The Day of the Locust*. The interior is a relief from the California sunshine outside, with dark-wood booths and a mural of a leafy New England in autumn. By all rights, I should order something authentically carnivorous and insouciant, like a rare steak and a gin martini, but it is midday in late spring, and I opt instead for a somewhat healthier Caesar salad with chicken, electively excluding myself from a true Musso and Frank experience. I speak too soon, because my waiter, Manuel, who has worked there for thirty-plus years, makes my salad from scratch right there at the bar, a courtly procedure involving a bowl wiped with a garlic clove, the flourished brandishing of a raw egg, and anchovy fillets. Throughout the theatrical preparation, Manuel continues his conversation with a woman sitting a few seats down, clearly a regular. The years have taken their toll and her back is curved over toward the wood of the bar, perhaps in a genuflecting tribute to the curling prawns in her cocktail. Osteoporosis hasn't dampened her spirits any. Her laugh is freely and frequently unleashed. It is the sound of rocks in a blender, a granite smoothie.

An afternoon rain has dispersed the tourists along the street. The gray light smoothes out the edges and polishes the street beautifully. As evening approaches, I take a taxi (un–thank you, Roosevelt) to see friends. The green Hollywood Hills rise just to the north of Hollywood Boulevard and the cab winding its way through the curving roads of Laurel Canyon is an antidote to the clatter of the street. The houses aren't the behemoth pleasure domes of Beverly Hills or Brentwood, but rather storybook sweet, with eaves overhung with flowering clematis. In the violet dusk, the vegetation seems to become an even more inviting velvet green, with the magenta bougainvillea and vivid red flowers of the bottlebrush trees standing out. It is all as calming and luxuriant as a Rousseau painting, the perfect break. When it is time to return later that night, the city lies just over the escarpment like a jeweled carpet. It seems so exciting that I can't wait to get back down the hill.

———

When I first got here, I found the breadth of the names of those enshrined on the Walk of Fame unutterably depressing, with its embarrassment of people who are all but unrecognizable. Every step was a cruel reminder of the heartlessness of time and tide. For every Hedy Lamarr to make you recall what a brilliant, patent-holding beauty she was, there is a Barbara La Marr to keep you cognizant that someday you, too, will be dead and the subject of a great, cosmic shrugging "Who?" (Barbara La Marr, "the Girl Who Was Too Beautiful," best friend of ZaSu Pitts, one of the first in Hollywood to succumb to drugs in 1926. She was already dead more than thirty years before they even started the Walk.) But as the days pass and I spend more and more time with the pavement, I revise my opinion. I suppose the way to think of it is as if the pipe-fitters union was honoring one of its own. It's just by happy accident that some of its members happen to be globally famous and recognizable. The custom has sprung up elsewhere—on Fashion Avenue in New York, I walk over Claire McCardell's and Norman Norell's plaques; in the Brooklyn Botanic Garden, that borough's native-born Ruby Stevens, better known as Barbara Stanwyck, has a paving stone among the greenery; on Toronto's King Street is Canada's Walk of Fame, about which 'nuff said. And in each place, the overriding sense one has is of, if not having intruded exactly, then at least being witness to something that ultimately doesn't involve one. A Walk of Fame by its nature turns out to be a very local phenomenon.

I take one last stroll over to Vine on my last morning on the boulevard. Most of the businesses are still shuttered. The tourists have yet to arrive at Grauman's. I pass by Dan Avey's star once again. It is all of four days old but I see that it is patched. No doubt, it left the workshop patched. There, against the salmon pink of the five-pointed star, is an occlusion of darker red, like a bruise or the small beating heart of a tiny creature. There is an almost animal frailty in that blemish that makes me stop in my tracks for a minute. People have been coming out West with stars in their eyes for so long, and for just as long, some have returned whence they came, their hopes dashed. But if one's dreams having to come true was the only referendum on whether they were beautiful, or worth dreaming, well then, no one would wish for anything. And that would be so much sadder.

III.
God's Country

"Great swarms of bees will arise. Are you ignoring the signs?"

The fortune cookie is nothing more than a canny History Channel promotion for a special about Nostradamus, but it seems an eerie message to receive mere days before my departure for Utah. Perhaps I am grabbing at straws by ascribing wisdom to a cookie, but the forty-fifth state owes much of its history to fiery-eyed revelation and prophecy, and Deseret—the original pioneer name for the territory—was a neologism Joseph Smith coined in *The Book of Mormon* to mean "honeybee." The beehive is even the state's symbol.

If the lobby of my hotel is any indication, the end of October is an auspicious time to visit, with the air abuzz with omen and augury. Arriving past midnight, I am greeted by an elaborate Halloween display of a dry-ice fountain, skeins of cobweb, and cutouts of Dracula and Frankenstein, made all the more ghoulish by overhead fluorescent lighting, like the nurses' station in a state hospital. My room is cheerfully located between the sixth-floor elevators. The springs of my bed wheeze. The elevator dings. The ice machine right outside my door rumbles forth its icy bounty, a steady tattoo that beats "Stay up! Stay up!" I am in a canvas that Edward Hopper never felt bummed out enough to paint.

Morning banishes the gloom. The air is sun-washed and pristine, carrying only a veil of haze from the California wild-fires that have been raging for weeks. The lobby is full of geneal-ogy tourists who have come to trace their family histories at the extensive Mormon archives. Utah, it seems, is where one comes to be found.

I join their happy ranks and follow them the few short blocks up to Temple Square, the spiritual and geographic heart of the city. A bride and groom hop up onto the stone ledge of a planter for the photographer, the better to capture the shining gold statue of the angel Moroni in the background. Moroni is the archangel of the faith, the prophet-warrior who gave Joseph Smith the golden plates that would eventually become *The Book of Mormon*. There are numerous couples in white dresses and tuxedoes marking their big day among the opulent glories of these world headquarters of the Latter-day Saints.

I begin in the South Visitors' Center, a sparsely furnished, carpeted space as hushed as a high-end rehab facility. The bulk of the displays are about the extraordinary and arduous efforts of the early Mormon pioneers in building the temple. Huge, rough granite blocks were hewn by hand, transported one at a time over miles in wagons that often broke under the weight of the stone.

"The Latter Day Saints labored with faith for forty years to build the temple. A flawed initial foundation, the arrival of fed-eral troops in 1858 . . . caused major delays." (An oblique refer-ence to the skirmish known as the Utah War when Washington, D.C., alarmed at the subversive and un-American practice of polygamy, sent soldiers in, replacing Mormon leader Brigham Young with Alfred Cumming as territorial governor.) Reading further, apparently the chief mason had his leg amputated and still managed to hobble the twenty-two miles to Temple Square and then climb the scaffold in order to carve the final, consecrating declaration HOLINESS TO THE LORD in the stone façade.

In his 1873 novel, *Around the World in Eighty Days*, Jules Verne sends Phileas Fogg and his valet, Passepartout, through Utah by train. There they encounter a man, dressed in the severe dark clothes of a clergyman, pasting flyers up and down the train. "Passepartout approached and read one of these notices, which stated that Elder William Hitch, Mormon missionary, taking advantage of his presence on train No. 48, would deliver a lecture on Mormonism in car No. 117, from eleven to twelve o'clock; and that he invited all who were desirous of being instructed concerning the mysteries of the religion of the 'Latter Day Saints' to attend." Passepartout takes a seat among thirty listeners. The elder William Hitch begins his heated oration "in a rather irritated voice, as if he had been contradicted in advance. 'I tell you that Joe Smith is a martyr, that his brother Hiram is a martyr, and that the persecutions of the United States Government against the prophets will also make a martyr of Brigham Young. Who dares to say the contrary?'" Hitch's outrage is understandable. Verne was writing less than fifteen years after the Utah War. Brigham Young had been imprisoned by the U.S. government for polygamy just the previous October. By the end of the jeremiad, Passepartout is the only one left listening.

Nearly a century and a half later, the Mormons remain objects of suspicious scrutiny, a reputation stoked by the likes of lunatic-fringe polygamist leader, convicted rapist (and, it should be noted, non-Utahan) Warren Jeffs. Or by the fact that blacks were only admitted into the Mormon church in 1978 (a divine revelation of racial inclusion that coincided a little too tidily with the recruitment needs of the Brigham Young University football team, I am told). A sampling of some of the other things about the Latter-day Saints mentioned to me over the course of my time in Utah:

- Polygamous houses are identifiable by the screening stands of cedars out front.
- Mormon housewives will "accidentally" throw a red item of clothing into the washing machine, thus changing their garments—the ritual underclothing that comes in standard-issue white—pink.
- There is a growing social problem in polygamous families where the patriarch—also known as the father—like a silverback gorilla whose sexual dominance is threatened, casts out the male children upon their reaching puberty. This is particularly common in households where some of the wives are young teenagers themselves. Facing homelessness, these adolescents fall under the care of the state or live in group homes, eking out livings as carpenters and cabinetmakers, part of the traditional LDS skill set.
- The usual proscriptions against caffeine do not apply to Coca-Cola, since BYU's board of trustees has a financial interest in the beverage company.
- There is a higher-than-average incidence of homosexuality among Mormon men. (This tidbit was always accompanied by a hyperlink to a calendar of shirtless missionaries and, like many theories in the "Who's gay?" phylum, almost invariably followed up with the

super-scientific assessment that "Mormon boys are the hottest.")

- The best place to see polygamous families is at Costco, where the competitive pricing and mayonnaise in jars the size of fire hydrants makes it the obvious choice for a household with eighteen children. Perhaps I went to the wrong one. I see nobody resembling sister wives. But far more miraculous are the free eats. Unlike the eagle-eyed young foodies who dole out the samples in New York, where they essentially memorize your face, thus making going back for seconds nigh on impossible, Costco SLC employs a (barely) standing army of the geriatric, the halt, and the mentally not-all-entirely-there, who man stations in their red uniforms and hand out free pizza, chiles rellenos, penne with chicken in "a quattro formaggio sauce," and never once give you the fisheye, even if you return in under a minute for another pleated paper cup of those excellent canned Indian River grapefruit segments.

Some of this is demonstrably true (Warren Jeffs *was* a polygamist and he *is* in jail; if social services is taking case histories from boys being thrown out of their homes, then QED), and some of it is essentially unverifiable (without proper LDS identification, you cannot even see the garments for sale in a Salt Lake City department store, white or pink). But it is the tenacity of and the pleasure taken in disseminating the whispered chatter that is remarkable. Prior to my trip, I did not fail to receive a joking "Don't let them get you!" warning from everyone I spoke to, as if I were marching into the waiting maw of a cult.

To understand why the Mormon faith might be routinely

tarred with the weird brush—and also why it should not—one need but visit the North Visitors' Center. The lower level is an unassailable and impressive testament to present-day Mormon initiatives, both local and global, for fighting hunger and doing good works. There are the requisite photographs of beautiful third-world children enjoying some all-too-rare nutrition or inoculation, although it is an unassuming pallet of canned food labeled DESERET INDUSTRIES, stretch-wrapped and ready for airlift, that packs the poignant punch.

Then, not twenty feet away, are interactive dioramas of scenes from *The Book of Mormon,* dealing with the prophet Nephi, a sojourn by the Nazarene Himself to the New World (there he is, blessing the Indians), and the Golden plates of runes revealed to and translated by Joseph Smith. In spirit, the particulars of the narrative are no more preposterous than the sagas that make up the cornerstones of Western society. This is not Scientology. Still, given this added liturgy and its narrative, found nowhere in the New Testament, it can be difficult to remember that Mormonism is a Jesus-based, Christian religion. (Over dinner, Morris Rosenzweig, a twenty-year resident, a composer and professor of music at the University of Utah in Salt Lake City, tells me of the time he was teaching a seminar on Bach and mentioned in passing the kyrie eleison only to be met by blank stares. A fairly observant Jewish man, late of New Orleans and New York City, he then had to stop and teach the components of the Christian mass to his Mormon students.) But Christ remains the fulcrum, as evidenced when one walks the circular ramp to the upper level of the North Visitors' Center. There, an eleven-foot-tall statue of Jesus stands in the center of a domed atrium. The walls and ceiling have been painted in a hallucinatory rendering of the universe not all that different from the backdrop of the Segway course in the Innoventions building at Disneyland. The lurid planets and surging nebulae may well reflect the Mormon cosmology, but they will also appeal to anyone who has ever been sixteen, attended a laser-light rock show at their local planetarium, or used *Dark Side of the Moon* as a rigid surface upon which to pick out stems and seeds.

The original, pioneer-era buildings of Temple Square—the Tabernacle, Assembly Hall, and Temple itself—are festooned with gold-rush frippery. With their Gilded Age flourishes and frontier-striver opulence of faux-marble columns and polychrome-plaster flowers, they are reminiscent of the Wheeler Opera House in Aspen, Colorado. At the northern extreme of the square, on the other hand, are two buildings that call up less benign associations. One is an imposing structure of white stone with square columns that would not be remotely out of place in Fascist Italy. Diagonally across from this Mussolini edifice is another huge LDS headquarters, this one a near parody of Cold War–era brutalism, with huge relief maps of the globe on either side of the massive doors. A Cheneyesque building that broadcasts an agenda of world domination. Neither do the church any public-relations favors.

A shame, and often not true. For decades, Mormon boys (and some girls) have spent two years overseas on missions as a matter of course. The undeniable facts of delayed black membership and an over-representation of LDS influence and funding behind California's Proposition 8, the state's anti-gay marriage amendment notwithstanding, there is also a cultural value placed on learning other languages and encountering other people, a concomitant lack of xenophobia, and a focus on the often-forgotten Christian notion of welcoming strangers into one's midst. On my way to the public library—an impressive Moshe Safdie–designed atrium for which the taxpayers dropped some serious coin—I am approached by an African American man who mistakes me for a resident and wonders if there wasn't once a building at a now-empty corner. He hasn't lived here for twelve years. He is back in town to find work as a cook, and is off to the library to work on their computers. "Oh, you've moved back," I say. "Not really *moved* back. Washington State didn't work out. California didn't work out. I'm back at square one." And Salt Lake City is about the best square one he can think of. That's a bit of a surprise, I tell him, given the church's only recent admission of blacks into its ranks. "That's *why*," he says, citing Mormon guilt as an explanation for the kindness. He has Mormon friends all over the country. The Mormons are good about treating people of color very well, he tells me. If they are so friendly and benevolent, has he himself become one? I ask.

"No way. That would be like joining the Klan," he says.

According to Mary Jane Ciccarello, a lawyer who deals with the elderly, Salt Lake City was once known as a welcoming city all over the West, to the point where other towns would give vagrants the bus fare and send them here. We are sitting in one of the hearing rooms of the Matheson Courthouse. We play peekaboo with a Hispanic boy seated in the row in front of us, a beautiful child of about seven, nestled in the arms of his affectionate father, a man of twenty-five at the oldest. The boy smiles at us throughout the hearings and fixes us with his enormous chocolate eyes. His father's left eye, by contrast, is occluded and milky with a neglected condition.

A very large young woman with a Polynesian name is called to the front (Salt Lake City boasts a sizable population of Mormon converts from Tonga). The public prosecutor is willing to lessen the disorderly conduct charge against her. He tantalizes us with just a hint of the actual story. "She was more the one who aided and encouraged, rather than actually the one who cut the hair."

A fellow in a county jail tan jumpsuit with greasy Wolfman

Jack hair comes out from the holding area. Mouthing "I love you" to his elderly mother, he faces the judge. He has meth and domestic-violence violations. He has failed to show up for court-ordered counseling or treatment. "Any reason we shouldn't revoke his probation and send him to jail?" asks the judge. The public defender mentions that his father is in ill health and it's not certain how much longer he will be alive. The defendant wants to "straighten up his life and fly right." But it seems he has had ample opportunity to do so on many occasions, the judge counters. His case manager stands up to address the judge. But even this angel of mercy is over it. She has tried everything. "He said he couldn't urinate in front of other people, so we did hair follicles and it was off the charts. It was nine times the limit. He should stay in jail and do the program there," she advises. The judge agrees.

"Put some money on my books," the man tells his mother as he is escorted out.

There are windows and natural light in the courtroom. The walls are decorated with framed artwork by children. But the cultivated dignity goes beyond the decor. The judge is respectful to all the defendants who come before him, almost particularly to those who jangle in, their progress hindered by leg irons. No one here is getting rich from doing this work, but there is none of the exhaustion, squalor, or apathy one generally associates with the court system. The proceedings are run efficiently by the clerks, two blond women who tap away at their computers throughout, scheduling hearings and return appearances, etc. Mary Jane pegs them as church members.

"No doubt about it," she says. "They probably have a ton of kids. The myth is that Mormon women don't work, that they're home being mothers. They all work. They have to."

Unlike some American Christian sects, for whom Halloween is a prime proselytizing opportunity, I am told that the holiday serves no similar purpose in the Mormon church, whose liturgy seems a good deal more heaven- than hell-based, as far as I can tell. Halloween decorations abound around the town in uncomplicated profusion. Even the Castle of Chaos, the local haunted house set up for the season, serves no evangelical purpose. Despite this year's theme of the Seven Deadly Sins, it is an entirely secular entertainment. Neither the horrors of abortion and its inevitable painful death from botched surgery and immediate dispatch to Hades nor the evils of predatory, recruited homosexuality and its surefire dividend of AIDS are among the creepy attractions.

The castle began in 2001 to serve as a departure from the usual Halloween fare, given the troubled times. "With the tragedies of 9-11, we gave an alternative to the gore and terror offered at other local haunts. For the past 7 years . . . our haunt has become more and more intense . . . Our actors are trained in theory as well as movement and interaction to ensure that you are immersed in not only the scares, but the reasons behind the scares as well . . . We are here to terrorize, yet entertain you. We are intensity," says its website.

The castle's façade of stone arches is painted on a plywood front attached to a one-story building out near the freeway. The thrash-metal hit "Du Hast," by a German band called Rammstein, splits the air: "*Willst du bis zum Tod der Scheide, sie lieben auch in schlechten Tagen?*" "Do you want to love her, until the death of the vagina, even in bad times?" (I *still* say Cole Porter should never have cut this from *Anything Goes* in New Haven.)

I head around the back to walk through the space and meet this cast of kinetic and theoretical adepts. Expecting a crack team of ninja therapists, or at the very least members of the Salt Lake City community of professional actors gigging for extra cash between regional productions of *Les Miz,* I find instead a group of kids under twenty, hanging out and smoking, wearing Goth teen-wear direct from Hot Topic, the mall franchise that has become the successful purveyor of prepackaged disaffection: black T-shirts adorned with safety pins and skulls, black pants designed with perpetually hanging suspenders. One boy has added a black cape in viscose, while another, who will be playing "Brian the Death Row Inmate," wears orange coveralls glazed with fake blood.

Climbing the wooden stairs of the loading dock, I enter the backstage area and approach the only grown-up there, thinking he is the evening's impresario, with whom I'd spoken on the phone. After a mere ten words exchanged between us, it becomes clear that I am speaking to a friendly but severely mentally challenged man. His role is that of a cadaver. When I ask him his name, he takes out some sort of Utah social services photo ID. "What *that* says," he tells me, pointing to the laminated card. Even though he'll be playing a corpse, he is wearing fake contact lenses, the irises eerily light-colored and disconcerting. Another boy, age fifteen ("I put people in coffins and send them down to their deaths in the chain-saw room"), is also wearing the fake lenses. His face is such a ruin of acne, a parody of adolescent skin, that I spend an interval wondering whether the star map of pustules has been applied like the eyes. I want to tell him that his pimples will be only slightly less temporary than the lenses, and that he shouldn't worry because underneath it all he has the face of an angel, but I know to say so would be much creepier than anything the Castle of Chaos could offer up. Instead I ask how much he's making. He diplomatically tells me, "*Some* of the actors get paid."

Outside the costume room is a list of rules, number three of which is "No inappropriate language." It makes me wonder what the fellow having the sickeningly realistic ax gash in his head perfected might say that could possibly offend. The castle experience, like all haunted houses, is set up like a journey. I take a brief walk through the rickety particle-board labyrinth and the words "fire hazard" ring through my ears. The plan had been to stay and hang out, to watch patrons get the shit scared out of them from behind the scenes, but it is all too much: the blaring German music, the simulacra of spattered crime scenes, the Victorian insane asylum-meets-Abu Ghraib menace of it all. I can't get out of there fast enough.

How is it, in this huge-sky landscape where just crossing the road is an airy jaunt that sings with openness and possibility, or is at least meant to, this place where one could start walking in any direction and just keep going, that I should have such a dispiriting sense of confinement?

It's a paradoxical feeling to have in the City of the Saints, since the streets of Salt Lake City are a steppe-like 132 feet wide. This breadth was decreed by Brigham Young so that a team of oxen and a covered wagon might be able to turn around in a full circle unimpeded. (An almost identical pronouncement was attributed to Cecil Rhodes when he was overseeing the layout of the city of Bulawayo in Rhodesia. Is this bit of hypertrophic urban planning just a standard issue paleo-Trumpism? One of the Seven Habits of Highly Effective Nineteenth-Century Men with Big Ideas?) The avenues yawn open, human proximity is vanquished, and the nearest people seem alienatingly distant. Such space between souls, such an uninterrupted vista of sky must imbue a populace with a sense of possibility—lebensraum and all that jazz. And yet, walking back to the car from the Castle of Chaos, I think of these teenagers, and they couldn't look more fettered—a world away from the crowds at the Gateway Mall, a bi-level outdoor shopping center constructed to look like an Umbrian hill town (if Umbrian hill towns had California Pizza Kitchens). If landscape shapes character, then it is never more clear than here, where I encounter the closest thing resembling a crowd in Salt Lake City. People, many of them in Halloween costumes, stroll eight abreast like one of Brigham Young's mythic team of oxen, never moving faster than the speed of cold honey. I have never been in a public space in America where a sense of how to walk among others was so completely and confoundingly absent. People stop abruptly, cut across lanes, and generally meander as blissfully unaware as cows in Delhi.

Perhaps it's not just space but the idea behind it that informs this entitlement. Human history has always been subject to the random and anarchic interactions of rock and water. Settlement succeeds or fails according to an unwritten checklist: Is there a felicitous dearth of malaria-bearing insects and wild animals? A convenient absence of marauding locals? Does that vengeful and quick-to-ire volcano god routinely incinerate our children and bury our homes beneath an infernal slurry of lava? No? Let's stay awhile.

Many places are colonized and consecrated in the name and glory of the Almighty, but what makes Utah unique, singularly so in the Americas, at least, is not just that those who settled it felt they *could* live there but that they *should* live there. It was upon receiving the reports from his advance men of this paradoxical region of arable land hard by an inhospitable desert and a crop-killing inland sea that Brigham Young then received the divine revelation that this was the true land of the Saints. Topography as God-given destiny.

And what topography! My friend Wyatt Seipp drives down from Idaho, and we head out of the city. Barely an hour from town, all is harsh and huge. We drive past the flaming smokestacks of oil refineries, past small towns in the foothills. For the non-alpine dweller, "foothills" seems an oddly reductive term for such incline and sky-blocking mass. The tiny houses nestle toylike against the slopes, and highest of all, by design, the local LDS temple, the golden pin dot of its Moroni statue gleaming.

We're heading for Promontory Point, home of the Golden Spike National Historic Site, about a hundred miles northwest of the city. It was there, on May 10, 1869, that the tracks of the Central Pacific line met those of the Union Pacific and were joined to form the first transcontinental rail system. The landscape is as large as the Golden Spike's museum/restroom/gift shop is inconspicuous and unprepossessing. It can be hard to fathom that we are at one of the most important places in the United States, but it was here at the Golden Spike that the country turned into, well, a country. The first transcontinental telegraph had been completed eight years earlier (in Salt Lake City, in fact) in October 1861, which was a boon to communication, to be sure. But you can tap-tap-tap "Mother ill. Come soonest. Stop" all you like, and if you're still relying on the stagecoach to get you to the deathbed in question, I'm afraid I have some bad news. The effect of the railroad was felt far more strongly and with shocking immediacy. This is not metaphoric. The Pony Express ceased operations two days later. With the railroads, the trickle of settlers coming by wagon train was suddenly upgraded to a flood of terrifyingly efficient westward expansion. Manifest destiny was transformed from the merely notional into reality at a speed never known theretofore. Just ask the Indians.

Scrub plain stretches in all directions to the suede-brown hills in the distance. Even seen from above, the satellite images on Google Earth reveal an expanse as beige and unvaried as a slice of bologna. One has a sense of how delayed the gratification of congress must have been for the Central and Union Pacific teams. No doubt, they must have had each other in their sights for weeks before they could consider the job done. Then again, the sight of anyone new, even if only in the distance, must have been a welcome tonic after months of laying track out in the middle of nowhere.

F. Scott Fitzgerald stopped too soon when he wrote about the fresh green breast of the New World (affectionately known as Long Island) that bloomed before Dutch sailors' eyes as being the last time man came face-to-face with something commensurate to his capacity for wonder. There was a whole continent beyond the eastern seaboard to slake the thirst of those seeking such adventure.

Standing at the squat commemorative obelisk, I try to conjure the mind-set that beheld this vast, sere pan of brown dirt—with the bare foothills rising in the distance and the far more forbidding gray, snow-capped mountains rising farther beyond, all under a sky whose unbounded immensity proclaims one's insignificance with an irrefutable and terrifying truth—but I cannot do it. How does one take all this in and *still* think, *Yes, I will go ever gaily forward. I will endure a pre-industrialized trek over hundreds of miles on a rocking, hard-slatted wagon bench, or in a saddle, or on foot. I will leave my children behind, or watch them succumb to scarlet fever, rickets, or infection. On those special occasions when I do wipe my ass, it will be with leaves. I will*

have an abscessed molar extracted by some half-blind chuck-wagon
drunkard wielding a pair of rusty pliers, and I will employ my own
just-past-Neolithic tools to make this railroad, this house, this town.
And one fine day, with my remaining *teeth, I will bite down on a*
leather strap while they amputate my leg without benefit of anes-
thetic and then I will hobble twenty-two miles on foot—one foot!—
so that I might then climb a scaffold in order to carve a tribute to
His glory into the unyielding granite escutcheon of a cathedral. How
did they do it? The monks and abbots who hauled the rocks to
build their monasteries on craggy Himalayan peaks and kept at
it until the job was done. Ditto the conquistadors who, even
fueled with the promise of gold, saw those jagged, stratospheric
peaks of the Andes and didn't just say, *Oh fuck this, I'm going*
back to Spain. It seems frankly remarkable that anyone anywhere
ever attempted anything.

Clearly—and history thanks them for it—people did. And
they have not stopped trying, either. We get back in the car and
drive about thirty miles south to Rozel Point on the northeast
shore of the Great Salt Lake proper, to the Spiral Jetty: Robert
Smithson's 1970 earthwork, arguably the most significant piece
of environmental art in the country, along with Walter de Maria's
Lightning Field in New Mexico. The directions, downloaded
from the Dia Foundation website, are exhaustively chatty. They
also warn us that the quality of the road diminishes precipitously
after the Golden Spike, and they're not kidding. Rutted and
dusty and cratered with potholes, Wyatt has to serpentine the
Jeep and slow down to such an extent that we eventually give up
and get out and walk the last bit.

The hills are littered with black basalt boulders. Below us to
our left the jetty projects out into the lake. Cue the screech-
ing brakes of dashed expectations. It's still an impressively huge
project, but the thirty-seven years since its construction have

not been kind. Its shape is barely discernible, certainly not the pristine fiddlehead fern the photographs would have one believe. Whatever whorl Smithson constructed is now largely lost; we think we make out a counterclockwise swoop but it stops well before another arc doubles back. And the whole is further diffused with random rocks and old wood pilings. Picking our way down the hillside, we resolve to make the most of it and walk along whatever portion of the earthwork we can still find.

The jetty's decay is a bit of a surprise. Given the meticulous stewardship of the Dia Foundation—to say nothing of their website which documents essentially every pebble that might fly up to the undercarriage of our vehicle—one would think there'd have been some warning or indication of the depredation of this, one of their jewels. It feels vaguely dishonest. The ingredients are all present and accounted for: the setting, the Great Salt Lake, black basalt. But it's like the Internet date who didn't lie, exactly; he *is* an underwear model, but for a prosthetics catalog.

We mask our disappointment with Pollyanna chatter about how fine the day, the relief to be out of the car, and similar platitudes. At one point stepping along the makeshift path, my feet sink down into the sucking mud. I pull my boots out with a terrestrial fart and soldier on with forced *Smell that air!* cheer. In the end, Wyatt's odometer will measure our journey at two hundred and fifty miles round-trip, and for what? A walk over crushed water bottles on sodden, uneven ground.

The day is a wash. We turn back from a good quarter of a mile out on this ruin and survey the shore. There, parked on the hillside, five hundred yards to our left, we see an SUV that had passed us earlier. And there down below, also five hundred yards over, two small figures quietly standing in awed silence beside Robert Smithson's perfect, sublime Spiral Jetty.

Oh.

I once knew of a Swedish piano student at Juilliard who spent his first six weeks in New York thinking that Americans were a bunch of delusional blowhards before he understood that the Statue of Liberty that was underwhelming him daily was a one-two-hundredth-size replica on top of a carpet store on the West Side of Manhattan.

There have, in the past, been years-long stretches when the jetty was submerged and largely invisible, but the water level has gone down, leaving in its place a hard-packed, blinding white tundra of salt. The gyre of ebony basalt couldn't be more beautifully visible, a black curl as pristinely contrasted on the salt sheet as a hair on a bar of soap. We are able to walk over and all around the 1,500-foot work on the surface of the lake, hard as solid ground in places, pleasingly slushy in others. In the distance, the roseate glow of the salt-loving algae makes a pink ribbon on the horizon. Smithson had likened the lake to a red Martian sea. The boulders of the spiral exposed to the windward side of the lake have taken on a tufted rime of salt, covered in small blunted protrusions; a stubby, thick fringe of sausage curls that make the rock resemble a line of sleeping lambs. Unyielding mineral rendered suckling-sweet. Like at the Golden Spike, the wind is a constant, cleansing hum on the ears.

The other couple moves silently about the jetty, taking long-exposure close-up photos of rock, puddle, and the supersaturated lake's crystalline progress that has built up in places to a cubic-zirconium size and brilliance. They don't say a word to Wyatt or me or to each other during the entire time we are there, although they occasionally bestow on us the almost drowsy half smile of the devotional pilgrim. The notion of pilgrimage was central to Smithson's vision of the work's impact. He chose Rozel Point because of its remoteness. As for the jetty's shape—a snapshot in stone of an unfurling galaxy—it spoke to his interest in notions of entropy. "I am for an art that takes into account the direct effect of the elements as they exist from day to day," he wrote. "Parks are idealizations of nature, but nature in fact is not a condition of the ideal . . . Nature is never finished."

Nor are we. Around us are odd bits of industrial detritus— a barely standing low concrete structure where we left the car, the decoy jetty we mistook for the real thing—all remnants of human effort, spinning out in ever-wider circles. Smithson saw it all as "evidence of a succession of man-made systems mired in abandoned hopes."

Smithson's right about everything except for that penulti- mate word, "abandoned." Maybe it's the unwavering brown that greets the eye, or the parching airborne salt one can taste on the breeze that jump-starts some atavistic impulse to defy such inhospitality and to shape this intractable land to our will. Look- ing around, it seems that aspiration might be the only thing that has not pulled up stakes here. The pioneers who founded Zion are long dead. The dust that was once those railroad barons has little need of the personal fortunes they amassed, but aspira- tion remains as green and tender as a lily stem. Even Smithson himself, devotee of atomizing dissipation, dead in a plane crash before the age of forty and gone from this earth for more than thirty years, constructed what might as well be a diorama of this unyielding faith. Newly emerged from decades of underwater obscurity, Spiral Jetty is now visible from space.

I Feel Dirty

The positive psychology movement began, in part, to address the perceived imbalance where the attributes of excellence at the upper end of the human spectrum were always being outshone by the negative. Society's greater respect for these lesser traits was baffling, it bordered on lurid fascination, and only served to bring the rest of us down.

Practitioners might take heart, then, from one arena. A vital and vibrant parallel universe where only the perfect survive: where the cable repairmen show up on time—early even—and are willing to go that extra mile; where the swim coaches, while stern, are also fair, with the benevolence and open-mindedness to consider a bargain with an athlete on probation who will do *anything* to stay on the team; where unmarried women have the self-possession and admirable self-respect to answer the door for the pizza boy wearing full makeup and heels, to surround their baths with lit votives, and to dapple the fragrant water with rose petals, even if no one else is around. Here is positive psychology made flesh. A realm devoid of frailty or failure.

It's nice to picture a world where even the most mundane encounter results in gymnastic, geysering, mind-bending sex. There is a reason that porn is a multibillion-dollar industry and documentaries are not. In a cinema verité world, one would have to think about what a pain candle wax is to scrape off porcelain, and how those rose petals are going to turn into mushy vegetable matter in about four minutes and just clog the drain. Or how the more likely cable-man scenario usually involves screaming "Fuck you, Time Warner! I take the day off work and your guy doesn't show? *Fuck you!*" into the phone. And surely no school would hire a coach who's clearly the same age as his athletes. Didn't they check his references?

According to the entrepreneur in a black double-breasted suit—what I will come to recognize as the uniform of choice for middle management in the adult industry—the contents of the slender steel can in his hand could transform even the coldest, most uncinematic reality, turning any day into my lucky one, if I knew what he was driving at. Only a fool wouldn't want to get in on the ground floor. His low-voiced talk is all about securing the American packaging and licensing rights to the obscure Chinese berry that delivers the tonic's unprecedented priapic oomph. Decades ago, he would have been a grizzled huckster, an old merchant seaman with fading Polynesian tattoos and missing teeth, producing from his rucksack a cork-stoppered bottle of brown glass. He would whisper of the mysterious contents, a vague pedigree of ground horn, dried animal penis, and the pulverized carapaces of rare insects.

The teamsters are running late and will not let us into Pier 94 on Twelfth Avenue. They are still securing the vinyl banner, as lurid pink and hot to the touch as a slapped face. It's an inauspicious beginning to New York City's first Exotic Erotic Ball and Expo. Starting on time seems the bare minimum to ask of an event featuring the titillating promise of ritual discipline— meted out with numerous leather crops, clamps, rubber horse bits, handcuffs (both regulation steel and marabou-trimmed), and ball gags—with a stage mocked up to resemble a medieval dungeon complete with a restraining device known as a St.

Andrew's Cross, and, eventually, numerous women punished for their nameless and hypothetical infractions by being variously ridden like oil-slicked ponies, spanked like recalcitrant children, and trussed up like a really good stuffed rolled pork loin I've made.

Then again, punctuality is less a moral virtue here than is Freedom of Expression. The term comes up in every single interview, conversation, and release. The ball began in San Francisco in 1979 as a campaign fund-raiser for one Louis Abolafia, who was running on the Nudist Party ticket, under the slogan "I have nothing to hide." (According to the press materials, it was Abolafia who also first coined the phrase "Make love, not war," although the most cursory Web search attributes it to sociologist-philosopher Herbert Marcuse.) In the ensuing years, the ball has gone on to become one of the mainstays of the Bay Area's legacy of libertinism, with official mayoral proclamations and the like. Past balls have featured the likes of Grace Jones, Joan Jett, and Kool and the Gang. For its New York debut, the organizers have scheduled a two-day trade fair to precede the Dionysian antics. The expo will have celebrities and vendors, along with seminars on how to become a performer, lectures on the current state of anti-porn legislation making its way through Congress, even a talk on pheromones. For the actual ball on Saturday evening, they have lined up all-around genius and musical innovator Thomas Dolby, as well as George Clinton and that living embodiment of the music-porn nexus, Tommy Lee.

Suddenly, wearing a flowered summer frock and exuding the freshness of every breathless ingenue who has ever come to New York to make a name for herself, she arrives, her heels making her pick her way over the shimmering asphalt. She stands there tentatively, placing one gloved hand—yes, short white gloves, just like Hope Lange in *The Best of Everything*—at the back of her head as if to secure the wide-brimmed hat she is not wearing. Craning her neck, she looks up and surveys the place that will be her home for the next two days. The only clues that she is doing this for our benefit—that she might be feigning her sense of wonder—are her vibrant no-carrot-found-in-nature-orange hair and her extraordinary better-living-through-surgery figure. That, plus the fact that Pier 94 is all of two stories tall. She should leave the pantomimed golly-gee-whizzums awe to the young Asian fellow standing nearby, who has arrived a touching two hours early. Ingenuous in equal and opposite measure where she is practiced, he is unable to close his mouth or tear his eyes from this display. Like an elevator gone haywire, his Adam's apple rises and falls in a cartoonish homage to the Jessica Rabbit proportions of her body.

"Is she a porn star?" another early bird asks me. A bearded amateur photographer, he is toting a large camera bag and elaborate equipment; he has cleared it with the expo officials that any pictures he takes will be for private use. I'm about to make some crack as how I actually think she's Madeleine Albright, but his attention is already elsewhere, following the backside of someone who *could* be Madeleine Albright: a sexagenarian Eileen Fisher–clad Mendocino art-therapist type (what magazine could she possibly be covering this for? *Tikkun?*). The mere fact that a woman has maybe had sex in her life—or might at some time in the future have sex again—seems to be enough to occasion neck-craning ass-spectatorship.

The erotic-tonic magnate's girlfriend slips me a can of the miracle stuff. I chug it to beat some of the heat in the parking lot. It's passably refreshing and raspberryish, and any worries that I'll be walking around with an irrepressible boner are allayed when she concedes that the drink's wallop is from good old caffeine, three cups of Java worth. Finally the doors open and we enter the vast space of Pier 94. After the midday sun of a June heat wave, the huge shed's highly effective air-conditioning is a relief. Out of nowhere, a small Chinese woman firmly places her hand at the small of my back, urging me over to the phalanx of those forward-leaning chairs in the corner of the cavernous space. "Massage! Massage!" she repeats. I beg off, mumbling something about journalistic impartiality but she appears to neither understand nor care. She has moved on. A true pro. I will not know it at that moment, but this is just about the most exciting thing that will happen over the next two days.

Carpenters are still at work, putting the finishing touches on a curtained-off area that will show vintage adult films at the ball. A workman is assembling the onstage torture chamber. Vendors have set up booths to hawk their erotic wares and services. Postcards are being fanned out, small baskets of chocolate kisses and single-serving lubricant are being set out on tables. The fifty-odd exhibitors are dwarfed by the ninety-thousand-square-foot room (this is only half of the building; it will be double the size for the ball). With so much unused space and with so few of us here, there is a depopulated-prairie-town languor to the proceedings, scored with the low hum of hushed conversation. After twenty minutes, I have visited every booth. After forty, I am on a nodding acquaintance with virtually everyone in the place. I look over the gags and paddles of a company called Ruff Doggie. The owner of a New Jersey sex shop, with the face of every Jewish girl with whom I ever Israeli folk-danced, pours a small amount of Porno Popping Climax Candy into my palm, gratis. I toss them back. Pop Rocks. I have world enough and time to examine the jewel-colored, jelly-rubber phalluses sold by Ricky's, a chain of New York drugstores that, rather than challenge the competition-killing kudzu ubiquity of the city's Duane Reade pharmacies, cannily reinvented itself as a dildo-and-boa emporium, catering to the needs of that Venn diagram of exaggerated and ghoulish femininity: drag queens and drunken bridal-shower parties. I spend a while talking arts and crafts with the latex-dress designer. I watch the feeble progress of a body painter as she (really poorly) executes a Puerto Rican flag on the hairy torso of her boyfriend. It's a little like being given a toy castle and realizing in short order that the flags on top of the turrets don't move, and the gothic windows, blue-water moat, drawbridges, all of it, is one piece: a dead end of rigid, injection-mold plastic.

Eventually, some 1,500 people arrive (that's the estimate of the organizers; eyeballing the crowd, I'd put it at about half that number), almost all men. They run a not terribly broad gamut of exurban-straight-white-guy phenotypes. There are outer-borough packs like the cast of *Entourage,* minus a famous meal ticket (sample T-shirt, YOU BETTER BUY ME ANOTHER BEER BECAUSE YOUR [*sic*] STILL UGLY). There's a cadre of tattooed motorcycle types, one of whose jacket reads IF YOU CAN READ THIS THE BITCH FELL OFF. Their dynamic is frosted with a homoerotic, gay-bashy, date-rapey menace. They jostle and spar and work one another up as they stand in line for autographs and have their photos taken with the various porn stars who are appearing. The undisputed number-one draw of the whole fair is a woman named Tera Patrick. An Internet superstar, apparently, she is part Thai and truly beautiful.

It's fascinating to watch the guys wait their turn. You've no doubt seen the loudmouth at jury duty. The one who snorts in short-fused disbelief at every instruction, or angrily rustles his newspaper, muttering under his breath while trying to catch your eye. He is the one who, at the first sign of conversation breaking out between anyone, immediately inserts himself and posturingly announces that he's just going to march right in there "and I'm just going to tell them, *I hate cops.* That's what

I'm gonna say, just like that, *I like rape, and I hate cops!,*" only to be cowed into respectful, truthful monosyllables by the solemn civic duty of it all when it actually comes time for his voir dire. At the moment the men reach the front of the autograph line, their horny, boisterous energy—all the muttered, snickering innuendo—dissipates and they stand there beside the objects of their desires, smiling shyly. I see no victory signs, no folded-arms gangsta posing. Few of them even dare to put an arm around the living object of their fantasies. And it's not just the magisterial beauty of Tera Patrick that's chastening them, nor even her tattooed bodybuilder husband standing nearby. Even Devyn Devine, "the Double D with the Triple D's," a sweet-faced dumpling of a woman with the proportions of the Venus of Willendorf, perched on her platform stilettos like a beer-can chicken awaiting the grill, a woman who could not seem less threatening, elicits the same audience-with-the-queen respect. There is one randy old retiree who continually tries to cop a feel, but he's so far out to pasture that no one really seems to care. Blond, buxom Brooke Haven—whom I immediately dub "Belle Laboratories"—smacks his hand lightly as it creeps toward her huge architectural breast with a good-natured, "Oh, you."

It's no wonder so many of these guys have come here in groups. Like anyone with a computer and an Internet connection, I've enjoyed a private, vicarious, frictive moment or two gazing at the erotic antics of folks far prettier than I (I do manage to put aside my dramaturgical skepticism now and then), but I wouldn't have the courage to attend an event like this *except* as a writer, and certainly not by myself. Admitting something like "I jack off to you. A lot" might make for a zesty and heartfelt testament of one's ardor to a loved one, but there is something simultaneously vanquished and courageous about saying it to a stranger, and the guys' presence on line, cameras at the ready, is tantamount to saying just that. It makes my young Asian friend seem that much more admirable for having come on his own. And I'm not overstating it when I say that it's lovely to see that he is getting such good return on his investment. Even after six hours, his face remains the same mask of almost reverential disbelief at his good fortune that it was the moment he breached the portals of Pier 94.

I have some sense of the hypertrophic attributes straight guys like in their porn stars: the hourglass far more than the test tube. Jessica Rabbit of the Parking Lot, for example. She has changed into a Lady Guinevere getup in red acetate and is giving out postcards advertising a line of topical unguents. (Arthurian romance is a fantasy mainstay but it requires formidable powers of imagination over and above the usual suspension of disbelief, given the current insistence in porn on an almost autoclave level of depilated sterility. Just think about the smell of two bodies, adhering to medieval standards of personal hygiene, coupling in sexual congress and try to keep your lunch down.)

Violet Blue is something of a departure from that model. A petite, twenty-nine-year-old with an almost ballet dancer's body whom one would never pick out of a crowd, naughty schoolgirl outfit notwithstanding. Even her walk is a purposeful, career-girl-on-the-move march rather than a siren's bump and grind. And still, she has more than three hundred and fifty titles in her filmography and is apparently a huge star. ("One of the top ten," says the correspondent for PNN—the Porno News Network—a human lipid of a man in a fuchsia silk shirt and, of course, double-breasted black *leather* suit. This is the man who, when I ask him if there is fraternization between members of the adult-industry press and the stars, skeevily clarifies, "There's fraternization between *friends*.")

She's here with her boyfriend, with whom she lives in Seattle. They left Los Angeles to have a somewhat more normal life for her six-year-old son. She is easing out of the business—her fiancé has made it one of the conditions of their eventual marriage—and she has made only a handful of movies this year (she gets paid by the scene, according to a sliding scale depending on the acts).

She is the youngest of nine children, "And I'm the *good* one!" she says. I tell her she's funny, apologizing if I'm stating the obvious. I've never clapped eyes on her before and have no idea if this is something for which she is also widely known. "That's okay," she says. "I've never heard of you, either."

I ask if her parents know what she does. "It would be kind of hard to keep this kind of thing from my parents." They live next door, in fact. "My mom altered my skirt for me," she says, standing up, showing the tartan kilt that has been abbreviated to little more than a pleated belt. "I LOVE MY PARENTS!" she cheers. I posit as how that might be a fairly unique narrative in this environment. She knows what I'm driving at: that people go into porn because they have lives of abuse and pain. It's presumptuous of me, to be sure, and she lets me know this gently, by saying, "I don't really know. I don't usually ask people how they get along with their parents."

Whaaaaaat?!?! It is this, more than the photographs of her introducing erect penises into her orifices, more than the images of models being double-penetrated or smiling for the camera with jism-glazed faces, it is *this* that I find most shocking. And no clearer proof that, although geographically still in Manhattan, I am visiting some alien principality that has nothing to do with New York City.

But everything is confusing about this event, right down

to its very name: Exotic Erotic. It conjures up notions of a no-holds-barred display of our richly colored tapestry of human libido, where anything goes. Freedom of Expression, as advertised. There is an extravaganza of women exposed to the male gaze, for sure, but beyond that, anything most emphatically does *not* go. There is nary a nod to female desire, and as for deviations farther afield, say, a reasonable expectation of a homo presence—especially with June's Gay Pride Parade looming just a few weeks away—it is limited to just one gay exhibitor: Lucas Entertainment, the porn studio owned and operated by Russian impresario Michael Lucas. Lucas is the Sergei Diaghilev of gay erotica, known for his high production values and array of impossibly perfect men. The table is spread with DVDs of Lucas's titles and model cards of his stable of stars, printed on one side with close-ups of their intimidatingly handsome faces and on the reverse with full-body shots of their equally flawless anatomies. Richard, the studio's national distribution manager, had been told there would be five other gay studios present. Instead, he has been a lone presence and a figure of derision since his arrival, when the guys working security called him a faggot. "This is New York City. It's not Utah, for God's sake. I almost jumped over the table to kick somebody's ass," he says. Still, he finds it amusing that when seated at the table he is largely kryptonite, but when he has walked the floor, he has been stopped by numerous men wanting information on how to break into the business.

There is even a panel discussion, moderated by Christopher, the guy in charge of public relations for the expo, about how to break into the business. This is, when all is said and done, a trade fair. Commerce is on many people's minds here. Christopher's co-presenters are the PNN correspondent and a meaty little fire hydrant of a girl named Cat, packed into a corset and black skirt. If this were Gilded Age New York, she would be the toast of Tammany.

The PNN guy gives the introduction. "Porn is a $6 billion industry. In porn, people work out of their homes. Their homes get bigger and bigger and their kids go to better and better schools." During his speech, just as at any panel discussion one might attend, Cat is kneeling at the edge of the stage, pushing her breasts together for a photographer.

Because the industry is so vast, he continues, with so many people clamoring to get themselves or their products noticed, breaking in is in large part about being able to write an effective press release. "I have to rewrite 99 percent of everything that comes in, except for Chris's stuff because it's damn near perfect."

"Thank you," says Chris with Sammy Davis Jr. humility. New York City has some fairly parochial proscriptions against public nudity and sex, so it is refreshing, after hours of relentless soft-core timidity, to finally witness a blow job.

Cat gives a lot of commonsense advice on how to make any kind of business call. She concedes that cold-calling can be difficult. "It's even hard for me on the phone when they can't see my boobs." I doubt that's true, actually. Cat is completely charming and funny. "Get straight to the point. People are busy. The first thing you should ask is, *Do you have time to speak to me?* Don't annoy people. If someone says they'll call you, you have to hear that and let them call you. But at the same time, your job is to make yourself seem like the best thing that's out there. Also," she finally advises, "this is *porn*. It's not brain surgery. Don't be afraid to get a little dirty on the phone. Crack jokes. Make it fun."

Make it fun. Advice worth heeding as I look over to the lounge area that has been set up with inflatable chairs. Two men are there reading car magazines. It is bus-station sad. A woman walks by, talking on a cell phone ("English," pause. "Technical support," pause). She idly taps a hand against her fake breast like she is drumming her fingers on a countertop. No, fun doesn't really seem to be on order at the expo, and it's not just joyless, gay me who seems to feel that way. I spot them from yards and yards away, mainly because of her flaxen, naturally curly hair, cornflower blue eyes, peasant shirt, and Birkenstocks. He has a fresh moon face. They are twenty-nine and twenty-six years old, respectively. She's an accountant; he's in the military, on leave from the Iraqi desert. They came down from Vermont for this, having seen a video of the San Francisco Ball via a friend who organizes passion parties, the suburban sex-toy equivalent of the old Tupperware get-togethers. They are disappointed, to say the least. They thought there would be more vendors, that it would be denser and more convivial than it is. They're not going to stay for the ball. "It doesn't seem worth it, and I don't have a lot of time off," he says. They'll drive back to Burlington this evening.

If only they had the leisure to take it all in like the older couple sitting in the café area, who wear looks of mellow amusement on their faces. She looks like Bella Abzug, right down to the hat. He, a man of at least seventy, is dressed in a polo shirt and khaki shorts. With tan skin and a brush cut, he is shuffleboard-ready. They are not a couple, actually. They just met here. "I was born and raised on the Lower East Side and I've lived in Brooklyn for the past thirty years," she tells me. "I came here because I like sex and I wanted to get back in touch with it. My husband died a few years ago." There is not a trace of self-pity in her voice.

He lives on Long Island. "On Monday, my son's girlfriend is going into rehab. She has four Emmys. She doesn't know what's about to happen. If my son doesn't clean up his act, he's going to have to go to rehab, too. I had to get out of the house. In my spare time, I hunt for pythons down in the Everglades. Did you see that picture of the python that tried to eat an alligator? We caught a python and chopped it up and fed it to the gators so they'd develop a taste for them and start to eat some of them. I have an eighty-eight-year-old pal who, for his birthday, I got him a hooker for a week. I partied with her all week during the day and he got her at night. For his eighty-ninth, I took him to Scores down in Florida."

Approaching the pier at 10 PM on Saturday, I meet a young woman with a wristband walking the other way. I ask if the ball is over already—it is scheduled to go until 3:00 AM. She's just off to get something to eat. She's volunteering in some capacity, which gives her free admission. I ask her how it is so far. She is very enthusiastic. "Oh, it's awesome! There are these gymnasts on a trapeze. It's really cool." My hopes up, I cross the West Side Highway and make my way through a murder of smokers in the parking lot. There are markedly more folks attending the ball than were at the expo and a healthy representation of women, but they are using the entire space for the ball. The pier is now double the size, and where once there were mere yards between people, it is, at 180,000 square feet, an absolute salt flat. Christopher the PR guy informs me that this is nowhere near critical mass. By midnight, the place will be packed and the big-name musical acts will be driving people wild. I hope for his sake he's right, because I can't imagine that this has been anything less than a financial fiasco.

The dungeon master is leaning against his restraining device, a St. Andrew's Cross: a simple wooden structure of two large X's, attached at the top like a sawhorse. He is eating some deli sushi from a clear plastic clamshell, but when he's done, look out! This is clearly the dinner break. A sexy angel and a sexy devil have to put down their takeout containers to have their sexy photo taken. Their mouths are still full, but at least they stop chewing for the picture.

The booths are all still open for business, but the space has been spruced up with an evening look, hung with large black-and-white-striped inflatable shapes: crescents, teardrops, and gourd-like biomorphic things. Three-dimensional and illuminated from the inside, they are beautiful and Venetian and playful and elegant, and they do indeed depend like brilliant jewels in the darkened air of the rafters. But at only seven in number, they might as well be a pair of cuff links decorating a stadium. There would need to be, at minimum, five times as many for them to even register. Similarly the acrobats, a woman flanked by two shirtless men in jeans, are as inconsequential as strips of flypaper. They move with the slowness of eucalyptus-drunk koalas, striking the occasional artful pose. One guy hangs by his ankles for about thirty seconds, while the other man seems to have given up before he has even begun and is just sitting twenty feet in the air. Perched above us for all to see, they act like a windsock, forecasting the conditions down on the floor. Tonight's weather: boring.

On the main stage, Violet Blue is performing a slinky dance in a black dress and feather boa to an all-brass version of the old Peggy Lee hit "Why Don't You Do Right?" She strips down to the boa and panties and garters, briefly flashing her small and natural-looking breasts. I understand why she has to limit her routine to these Olde-Timey, hoochy-koochy moves, disallowed as she is to be naked in public. But I don't get why people who have seen Violet Blue perform the most unbridled sexual deeds are settling for this Vegas-style all-you-can-eat-salad-bar floor show. Perhaps the thrill lies in the very incongruity of Violet Blue herself.

She doesn't exude even the faintest whiff of sluttiness, *especially* as she gyrates the twin kidney beans of her tiny ass.

Tera Patrick, the undisputed star of the whole thing, also strips for the crowd. Occasionally she will stop and cock a hand to her ear in an "I can't hear you" gesture. The crowd—about seventy people—cheers. Her fake breasts are mathematically perfect circles. They mesmerize the men in some preverbal way, like newborns who see the archetypal configuration of facial features in an electrical outlet.

The emcee appears onstage: "Now comes the time in the evening that we call Lesbian First Kiss. Is there a girl in the audience who's never kissed another girl?"

Ah yes, the "lesbian kiss," one of the building blocks of straight porn. Three women from the audience volunteer. One is a Yale scholar in bioethics, another is a botanist studying the rapidly disappearing Belizean rain forest, and amazingly enough, the third works for an NGO trying to bring potable water to sub-Saharan Africa. Just kidding. There is Goth Girl in torn black hose, Belly Dancer in a gold brocade bra and harem pants, and Platinum Blonde in revealing white satin. Their kisses are gestural and disingenuous, all open-mouthed fluttering of tongue against tongue.

Just behind the stage is the VIP area, replete with such extra-ritzy accoutrements as folding chairs and inflatable loungers. A mandala of cheese slices has been picked over and is curling up at the edges. On a little platform, a pasha ties up Belly Dancer. Her descent into turpitude has been quick; from first lesbian kiss to seraglio prisoner in just ten minutes. He is a tentative and unpracticed despot. The process is taking too long, the methodical steps and knots requiring such a docile and unmoving victim, that it renders the entire need for restraint moot. It is as gripping as watching someone make pierogies. Standing beside me is a Viking, his Nordic-marauder realness belied by Coke-bottle glasses. Outfitted in a helmet with plastic horns and a brown cape made from his plush fur bedspread, the years since his *Star Wars*–themed bar mitzvah melt away as he takes in the proceedings with a face of innocent delight. Today, he is truly a man.

People paid an extra forty dollars to get back here, where approximately nothing extra is going on. Walking back into the general area, I see a man looking as longingly as Moses must have gazed at the Promised Land he was forbidden from entering. I quickly disabuse him, telling him he's missing nothing, that it would be like blowing all his frequent-flier miles on a first-class upgrade to Grand Rapids, but he is having none of it. *Somewhere, somebody* is having a sexy, fun time that he cannot see. I know just how he feels.

Midnight. What should be the height of the ball. A *Moulin Rouge* spoof up onstage is an amateurish, unsynchronized can-can. At the dungeon, a sleepy torturer desultorily flicks his horse-tail whip on the back of his victim, shooing away imaginary flies. She is tied up like a piñata. A man at the side of the stage is talking to her and joking and then tickles her under the chin repeatedly. Tied up as she is, she is powerless to stop him—which is, I guess, kind of the point of a dungeon—but her official tormentor will not brook any unsolicited harassment.

"Dude, leave her alone, I'm serious," he says.

One summer, while in college, I worked on a chart review of schizophrenics, amassing data on first onset of disease, nature of each episode, adherence to medication protocols, etc. What never failed to astonish me was how the patients, people who had supposedly been cut loose from the moorings of rational human behavior, were all getting messages transmitted from the radio or television directly into their brains, or their metal fillings were telling them to stand outside the Israeli embassy in their underpants. They all started to look like conventional strivers in some homogeneous psychotic suburb. Voices in the refrigerator? Get in line.

Things seem similarly canned and derivative here at the ball. I see the same white pleather nurse's outfit over and over again. What *is* this fascination with nurses? I owe my very life to nurses, for sure, but has no one ever been woken up out of sleep in the hospital only to then be given a sleeping pill? Or had their IV tubing back up with blood? Or had a catheter put in—and then, dear God in heaven above—taken out? A Joe Pesci type stands in motorcycle boots and leather codpiece. One of the few men here in costume, he looks mildly confused, as though he'd been chloroformed, stripped, and dropped off. Holding his bundled street clothes under one arm, his car keys glinting in his fist, kind of ruins the effect, but God love him for trying. It's hard to ignite a sense of collective passion in a crowd where the nearest person is twelve feet away and where only a quarter of the people are dressed up. Even the sexiest of getups is powerless when outnumbered three-to-one by a boner-quashing sea of Dockers, or the bespectacled Bill Gates minus the billions in his molded white plastic George Lucas stormtrooper costume. People seem bored. They barely register the sword-swallower doing his bit to inject some neo-vaudevillian sideshow sordor into the proceedings, and they perk right down with the act that follows him: a troupe lip-synching the numbers from *The Rocky Horror Picture Show,* a film released before most of the performers were born. Moreover, the material's mid-'70s tolerance and polymorphous perversity are actually a little gay for this crowd. "Wasn't that great? You can see it a thousand times, and even on the thousand and first, it's still just great," the emcee praises backhandedly.

Thomas Dolby takes the stage at close to 1:00 AM dressed in WWI flying-ace gear—goggles, headphones, double-breasted olive-drab trench coat. He is putting on a hell of a show, but for a skeleton crew of twenty people. Here's what I do not see in all my time at Pier 94: vomit, major drunkenness of any kind, a fight, a couple going at it, anything resembling an erection, clothed or naked. At 1:30, a doughy, shirtless boy in khakis is being worked over by two dominatrices up on a small stage, but their torments are of the gnat-like schoolyard "got'cher nose" variety. The place lacks that up-too-late spirit of abandon, the grand erotic gesture that one will doubtless regret in the morning but which one does anyway.

If I stay any longer, I will be the only one left and they'll probably make me help clean up. I catch a cab on Twelfth Avenue and head home.

I have always tried to be the kind of New Yorker who can simultaneously decry the hideous corporate annexation of the city without getting misty-eyed over a time when an underage runaway girl could abase herself for a bunch of leering patrons in a Times Square peep show. I'll admit that it saddened me when I first heard that New York had to import something like the ball to get its groove back. Had we collectively become such a bunch of super-egotistical milquetoasts that we were looking to Northern Californians to be our wizards of id? We seem to be at an age, both personal and historical, where sex can only answer for so much. As unimpeachably true as a statement like "Make love, not war" may be, it also feels quaint, the reductive naïveté of a bygone world. Even Perry Mann, who founded the ball back in 1979, has taken a break from having sex for the last two years and, although born Jewish, has become a regular churchgoer, too. "I've had threesomes, foursomes, orgies, and I've stepped back. It's interesting. I look at people and things in a different light."

All the Time We Have

Many are the tears of grief—there are those who might even say the majority—that fall for no one but the one who is shedding them. A literary agent I knew, his AIDS-related symptoms escalating daily, decided to retire from the business and make a graceful exit before his final reckoning. He called up his clients to tell them he was, in essence, dying, and one of his writers, his eardrums barely done trembling from the sound waves of this news, responded with an immediate and lachrymose, "But who's going to represent *me*?" Would that this was even fractionally as aberrant as it is appalling. At the memorial service of *another* literary agent, a giantess in her field, one of her stars—a mystifyingly, wildly successful children's book author with a penchant for neo-feminist retellings of fairy tales and a cloying, breathless prose style, given to phrases like, "*O, but how she did run like the wind!*" and "*stealing out into the darkling night with naught but a loaf of wheaten bread and a flagon of ginger beer*"—found it charming to tell the assembled crowd that her six-year-old granddaughter, upon hearing of the death, responded with a wailed, "But she was going to be *my* agent!" I kept these cautionary tales in mind when I made my way to Beth Israel Medical Center to visit Del.

Del had been my therapist. His efforts in my behalf were Herculean; he earned every dollar I ever paid him. I had been a chilly and resistant analysand from the start, although I stayed with him for ten years. I once admitted to a woman at a dinner party that I had never once cried in therapy.

"Never?" she asked, astonished. "Your therapist is no good."

"No, my therapist is very good, but I'm better," I joked.

That I was ever able to extricate myself from my day job and become a writer was largely thanks to Del. The debt I owed him was unpayable. Even so, when I finally quit, the thought that I might never see him again was only mildly troubling. The very notion of post-treatment contact struck me as inappropriate. Having grown up surrounded by psychiatrists, I lack that general curiosity people seem to have about shrinks, or their own shrinks, at least. From a very young age, I can recall being out in public, and seeing my father stop suddenly, or if we were sitting at a table, subtly turn his back to the restaurant and face us, an attempt to not be seen by a patient. Sometimes it was unavoidable and an efficient hello might be exchanged, but we knew, my siblings and I—notwithstanding the eager smiles and eyes that raked over us like searchlights—that we would not be introduced. These were not social interactions, and any questions we might have had would emphatically not be entertained, although I can't recall having any. Chalk it up to time and place, the 1960s and early '70s in Canada, where a British reserve still overlaid society. Things were different in New York, I have been told. The membrane between shrink and patient was more permeable. That still seems to be the case. Once, at a birthday party for a friend, her former psychiatrist got up and sang a Joni Mitchell song to all assembled. Putting aside the romantic declaration of the lyrics, "I want to knit you a sweater, Wanna *write you a love letter!*" (appalled italics my own), it just seemed improper.

I could never really get with the looser program. There were aspects of my relationship with Del that played out in the usual transferential manner—the craving for his approval, the briefest flashes of displaced anger on my part—but that classic desire for intimacy didn't really come up for me. I didn't hunger for details of Del. I was never moved to Google him (or as we used to call it back in 1989 when I started treatment, "look him up in the phone book"). I gleaned things about him over the years without trying: he was from Omaha; he had a Jewish father and had been raised in a Jewish household, but had seen fit to formally convert in adulthood (I translated the Hebrew of a rabbinical document he showed me); he had been a practicing Buddhist for years. I even found myself marching behind him one year during Gay Pride (that was not a bombshell; I had gone looking for a gay therapist from the beginning). He looked back and smiled. There was no internal flutter, like when as a child I would see a beloved teacher beyond the confines of the classroom. I didn't even take the opportunity to see who he was marching with. The moment seemed nothing more than ripe for a joke. "It's my shrink," I said to my friends. "Quick! Knock me to the ground and pee on me!"

Not long before we decided to terminate—no doubt exhausted by years' worth of pulling teeth and scoping around for some last-ditch tactic to crack me wider than I'd theretofore allowed—Del started to employ that old reporter's trick of disclosing things about himself in hopes that I might finally, monkey-like, proffer confessions of my own. With a defiant regularity, he began co-opting our conversations. He extolled the benefits of acupressure and how it cured a bowel obstruction he'd had (*ick*). He mentioned a recent trip to Cuba and how beautiful the men were, although "We figured they were mostly hustlers," he added (I did not inquire who the "we" was). Once, when I was leaving, he even told me that my blue shirt was doing "wonderful" things for my eyes. All to no avail. Finally, he stopped me one day mid-rant about being broke. "David, I'm between a rock and hard place here. I hear and understand your anxiety about money, but we have something like seven sessions left and we have to at least talk about your leaving."

Turning things around, I asked him what his feelings were about our ending things. "I'm incredibly angry," he responded fondly. "How dare you? You should at least have to come and have coffee with me once a week." I asked if he felt this way about most of his patients. "Not really," he responded.

(Sigh. Should you happen to be possessed of a certain verbal acuity coupled with a relentless, hair-trigger humor and surface cheer spackling over a chronic melancholia and loneliness—a grotesquely caricatured version of your deepest Self which you trot out at the slightest provocation to endearing and glib comic effect, thus rendering you the kind of fellow who is beloved by all yet loved by none, all of it to distract, however fleetingly, from the cold and dead-faced truth that with each passing year you face the unavoidable certainty of a solitary future in which you will perish one day while vainly attempting the Heimlich maneuver on yourself over the back of a kitchen chair—then this confirmation that you have triumphed again and managed to gull yet another mark, except this time it was the one person you'd hoped might be immune to your ever-creakier, puddle-shallow, sideshow-barker variation on "adorable," *even though you'd been launching this campaign weekly with a single-minded concentration from day one* . . . well, it conjures up feelings that are best described as mixed, to say the least.)

At the end of our last session, I stood up to leave and put out my hand. "No way," he said, and pulled me into an embrace. In our ten years of acquaintance, it was the first and only time we ever touched. Bills, breath mints, money had all passed between us in hermetic and sanitary noncontact. I was shocked to find that he was shorter than me.

There is that archetypal moment in a women's film, where a title card reading "Three Years Later" comes up and then you see the protagonists—a little wiser, with incipient crow's feet, their hair a little duller perhaps, their clothes most definitely better— meeting across a table at '21' or the Biltmore Room where they bring each other up to date on all that's happened in the intervening time since all of their dreams came true (or did they?). I wrote and dedicated a book to Del, and mailed him a copy, but I had already heard through the grapevine that a virulent and aggressive colon cancer had forced him to close up his practice, seemingly within a matter of a few short weeks. He was very moved, but he begged my indulgence; he had little energy or focus for reading. He was already in hospice care at Beth Israel, although he sounded positively cheery on the phone. He would love a visit. I asked if I could bring anything and without hesitation he asked for two Budweisers, a Big Mac, large fries, and a Diet Pepsi. His last hurrah. I was reminded of the only true fight we ever had.

He had once asked if he could eat during a session. I didn't care. I saw him at the end of the day, he didn't have a moment to himself. Del's supper was a Tupperware container of unhulled grains and some dark, leafy greens. If a Joan Baez song could be food, this was it; a sad and earnest cloacal scouring pad of a meal. This was around 1991, a period during which I was spending a good amount of my time shuttling back and forth among New York's AIDS wards visiting sick friends. I made numerous shopping trips to the Integral Yoga store on Thirteenth Street where I would root around in the bins of grimy vegetables for exactly these ingredients for one friend who was piebald purple with Kaposi's lesions. I asked Del if everything was all right with his health.

He didn't mind that I would ask such a question, but he took issue with the way I asked it. I thought I had invested my voice with a calm assurance and a let's-not-worry-until-there's-something-to-worry-about unflappability. To his ears, I had sounded clipped, harsh, and unforgiving. I had always appreciated my own oncologist's English stoicism and distaste for sowing false hopes (a man who, when at the age of twenty-two I asked him if my impending chemotherapy would have side effects, responded with a bright-eyed, "Oh yes. It's profoundly nauseating. You'll be vomiting within half an hour"), or my erstwhile New York GP whose bedside manner was borderline-actionable and hilarious. A man who would say during every rectal exam, "Bet this takes you back."

As I recall, Del and I reached a chilly détente, each acknowledging the other's different verbal style, but neither of us giving an inch.

McDonald's bag in hand (I would have brought him a Cuban hustler if he had asked me), I arrived at Del's room on a sweltering summer day. He was on the phone. More metastases than man, tipping the scale at ninety pounds maximum, he was sitting up in bed, his underpants gaping around the tops of his emaciated legs. I'd stopped being shocked by that change in appearance. Perhaps years of having seen friends diminish to skeletal shadows of themselves inured me. Or perhaps it had more to do with the very odd nature of our bond.

"Hi, David," he said, handing me the phone to return to its cradle (those words always had an avuncular, almost regretful falling intonation). "You look good," he said, appraising me.

"Actually, I take that back. You look fine but there's a slight reserve, a kind of sadness there." I gave him a *No shit, Sherlock* look, which made him laugh. I poured his Diet Pepsi into a small cup and stirred it to get the bubbles out. He slowly unwrapped the hamburger, took a tiny bite, chewed it for a few seconds and then discreetly spat it out into a napkin. His interest in the food was gestural at best. He could no longer digest solids. His systems were breaking down. He was to be fitted with a PIC line later that day, a port that bypasses the smaller veins and lets the pain meds go more directly into his system. All of these were signs that he was "getting closer," as he put it. "And I have to deal with that emotionally," he said.

For the next three hours, I fell into my preferred hospital-room function of bustling around, picking things up, replacing the ice in the pitcher, delivering the cookies I made in his behalf to the nurses' station, deadheading the flowers. He catnapped and we talked. He expressed some mild regret—what can only have been the merest tip of a ship-splintering iceberg—that he hadn't traveled more. "California! I went there and thought, 'This is marvelous! One really needs a month here to explore this place properly.'" He had desperately wanted to go to Italy, but delayed two critical weeks until he was too sick. "But I saw Tibet," he said. (This was all a surprise. As a resentful twentysomething, filled with rage, I had constructed an angry fantasy of this man getting rich off of my dollars, financing country houses and numerous trips abroad with moneyed abandon, while I scraped together my pennies so that weekly I might enjoy the dubious privilege of dredging up feelings I'd rather have kept tamped down.)

Later in the afternoon, I don't recall how it came up—I certainly didn't ask—he mentioned as how he was planning on being cremated. "A friend of mine knows a place in Florida where

Krishnamurti might have once been, so I'm going to have some of my ashes scattered there." As for the rest of him, the implication was that whatever was left over after this Panhandle Hegira didn't really concern him.

Where Krishnamurti *might* have been? There was something so utterly bleak about this disposal, being cast into an apathetic wind in a place whose significance was little more than a matter of conjecture. The relinquishing of craving and thereby achieving detachment is perhaps the noblest of the Four Noble Truths, I know, but I wanted nothing more than to take him in my arms and moor him to the here and now. This all felt like some obstinate standing on principle on his part, the spiteful child taking leave of a world that he felt had cared about him insufficiently. Del would have said I was projecting (as would anyone, frankly). I didn't know anything about his life to justify this conclusion, but I wished that I could turn to those closest to him and say, "Talk some sense into him. Tell him how much we love him." That I might have told him as much myself only occurs to me now.

A nurse came to check his diminishing vitals, along with someone from his temple who was going to say some prayers. They drew the curtains around him and I stepped out into the hallway.

Searching through literature on therapists' deaths and its effect on their patients, I came up with scant material. One analyst, in introducing his article on the subject, wrote, "A few heroic analysts have described their work in the face of life-threatening illness. However, there are only limited descriptions of these illnesses and deaths from the patient's point of view. Experiences of less heroic colleagues are almost unavailable." That he would characterize as less than heroic the tending to one's own impending death—whether by having one's days filled with the projectile expulsion of vomit, bile, or God knows what else until one is an empty sac of lifeless meat, or the pre-morbid twilight of a pain-masking morphine drip or a PIC line, or by simply having the narcissistic, cowardly gall to buy the farm by sailing through a windshield and scrambling one's brains on the pavement, with nary a thought given to one's patients—was precisely what I found so troubling when people said, "That must be very intense for you," when I told them that Del was dying. It was. I suppose. It is always intense to lose someone, and Del was an unbelievably good egg. His being under fifty-five seemed doubly unjust, and he had quite literally saved my life, to boot. But given my decade's worth of egocentric monologue, would I be grieving a man or the imminent demise of a reliquary of my deepest pains, most artful observations, and wittiest bon mots? Was I mourning the cancellation of the David Show ("Who's going to represent *me*?")? I didn't feel entitled to that particular hue of despond.

Outside of Del's hospital room, I listened to the low chanting of sutras. There was a framed copy of the New York State Patients' Bill of Rights posted on the wall. It was written in English and Spanish, and also Yiddish. Rosetta-stoning with the English translation at the top, I read through the text. In about five years' time, I thought, this version would no longer be relevant, even at a place like Beth Israel. An era was passing.

After about thirty minutes, Del's friend came out to tell me he had fallen asleep. I went home. I would not see him again.

A day or two later, the following dream just before waking: a phone call from Del. "Hi, David. I'm much better, and in fact we're to meet for dinner at seven just around the corner. The head of oncology will be there, too." And suddenly there he is, only now he is a small boy, no older than six, fresh from a bath, his black hair wet and combed (between Del and myself, only one of us has dark hair and it isn't Del). Wearing light blue pajamas, he climbs onto my lap. "Look," he whispers, unbuttoning the jacket. The pale skin of his chest is marred by something, a tattoo, or a wound, or a scarification. Whichever it is, it is clear this injury is a devotional mark. Incised for my benefit, it is a bruise of allegiance that would be carried forever.

Another Shoe

Vanity, thy name is Matt. I think. (I had dubbed him "the Sleeping Statue" early on, for the beauty of his sculpted form and his perpetually heavy eyelids that made it look like the perfume of his own perfection had drugged him. After the day he said hello, I renamed him "Garbo Talks.") His very presence in the gym was a rebuke. With my mid-forties looming and the corpus an unsightly ruin of a thing, I went each morning and, in grotesque imitation of the Sleeping Statue, lifted my weights while I stood wobbling on a half ball like a poodle in a dog act.

The effect was almost immediate. Within days of the new regimen, my left thumb and forefinger started to tingle and go numb, a feeling I could dial up or down just by turning my head. Mere days after that, the tingling and numbness graduated to a pretty constant pain. I had pinched a nerve in my neck. I could almost see it: a protuberance poking out from between my disks, a tiny balloon twisted tight into a tense and angry bubble. The more I exercised and stretched, the worse it got. Gone were my dreams of aesthetic payoff and now I was just looking for relief. For the better part of eight months, I jolted out of sleep every night between 2:00 and 3:00, woken abruptly as if someone had poured gasoline over my left arm and lit a match. Running my hand under cold water helped a little, but only for the time I stood at the sink. What scant sleep I got was a matter of rocking back and forth on the couch until dawn, when exhaustion finally gave me an hour or two. I became useless with my circadian rhythms shot. The only upside was when I traveled to Australia for two weeks and experienced not a moment's jet lag.

"There's bad wind in the arm," said the acupuncturist. "You should take a hot bath." I have no tub in my apartment and at that point, it was a little bit like being asked where on my gunshot wound would I like my Barbie Band-Aid. I had tried everything, and none of it provided any relief beyond the duration of its administration. The physiotherapy; the electrical stimulation, involving sticky pads and a dial that could administer effervescent mild shock waves; the X-ray-guided cortisone shots directly into my neck; an expensive massage; the Eastern medicine . . . all of them, while okay in the moment, hadn't worked. The physio doctor, out of options, in an effort to see what, if anything, was in there that was causing so much pain, scheduled an MRI, a claustrophobia-inducing procedure that I had managed to avoid my whole life.

At eight years old, in the Canadian Rockies and faced with the prospect of an enclosed gondola that traveled up to the summit of a mountain, I wept in fear, as I was often wont to do, even as I understood myself to be in surroundings of unconscionable majesty and loveliness; magnificent peaks rising through the pine-scented air, with adorable, nut brown chipmunks scampering about. After what must have been a trying interval of patient parental psyching up, I finally marshaled myself and got on. In the snack bar at the top, tears all dried, my father made me a medal in one of those machines that presses letters into a metal disk—part sheriff's star, part one of those plastic cogs one used to put over the central post in a turntable to play a 45. DAVE

THE BRAVE it read. Everything about it was counterfeit, from the rhyming slogan's required shortening of my name into the falsely masculine Dave, to the lightness of the cheap, soft aluminum, too easily impressed—more thumbprint cookie than Vulcan-struck ingot. It could have been a mirthless joke, given the surface falsehood of the inscription, but it turned out to be a counterphobic talisman. If something was frightening, the fear itself was reason enough to do it.

Dosing myself with enough tranquilizer to fell a horse, I managed to climb into an MRI machine, getting through the scan by silently alternating between singing "Court and Spark" by Joni Mitchell and reciting Elizabeth Bishop's "Letter to N.Y." in my head, both of which were the perfect length and afforded me some distraction from the fact that I had been slid into a highly magnetized coffin. Kudos to phobic little me. The next day, I sent the long-suffering technician a bottle of bourbon, so guilty and grateful was I.

Grateful for what, I am not sure. In my characteristic stupidity, I had confused the taking of the test with the result. I danced around the city like an idiot, out of jail, feeling brave, effective, free! The doctor called to tell me that it *was* a pinched nerve, but it was being pinched by a six-centimeter mass.

The oncologist palpates the area and sends me for a needle biopsy to see if they can extract any cells. Two doctors plunge fine sharps into my neck where they think the mass is, but the points come out clean and acellular, as if they'd tried to extract fluid from a pencil eraser. This is very good news, apparently. Lymphomas can be juiced like ripe tomatoes, I am told.

"I'm happy for you," says the oncologist. Uttered as they are by a man whose job it is to sometimes deliver horrible news of the most hopeless kind, I take his words immediately to heart. I'd had lymphoma in my early twenties and was worried that it had somehow come back, but I am only a tourist here, after all! I gather my things with an air of impervious superiority, like a coach passenger whose upgrade to business class has just come through. A mother and father wheel their grown son into the waiting room from the suite of offices behind the closed door. The son appears to be in his late twenties, but disease has swollen his face into an angry red, almost Asiatic Brezhnev mask. The news has not been good and all three are crying quietly. The son manages to maintain vocal control as he says to his mother, "I only care that you're okay." She responds with an equally brave, "And I only care if *you're* okay." The father's eyes are wobbly with tears. If he makes a move, it is clear he will fall apart. It is hard to witness and I'm a little choked up as I remit my $25 co-payment, but I recognize in my incipient tears the remove of spectatorship and the joy in that which separates us. There is nothing so cleansing or reassuring as a vicarious sadness. This is precisely why I never went to talk to a cancer group when I had Hodgkin's disease. It was the heartless mathematics that kept me away. I didn't want to provide the charm of contrast to those less sick than I was, and I didn't want to subject others to my own silent but unmistakable "Well at least I'm not *you*" relief. Scientifically baseless though it may be, if your chances are one in ten, you will derive a predatory comfort from the presence of nine other souls facing a similar numbers game. I could only envision us as serving as one another's wounded gazelle, the member of the herd most likely to fall behind and take one for the team when the lions attacked, as if someone else's misfortune could inoculate one from circumstance. It was all a little too Agatha Christie for me.

I go to a neurosurgeon who confirms the oncologist's initial high hopes and speaks of the ease of the procedure to rid me of my so-trifling-as-to-be-nearly-nonexistent afflic-tion. It's a nerve sheath tumor, nothing more. He sees them all the time, and they're almost always benign. Even the name, schwannoma, delights me, sounding as it does simultaneously Native American and Yiddish. *Benign even in patients with previous histories of cancer?* I ask. Yep, I am assured. We sched-ule surgery for early December. I do not tell my parents, look-ing forward to the day when they will see the by-then healed scar and I can say, "Funny story . . ." I cook Thanksgiving for ten people, and days later walk into the operating theater. After a brief night in the hospital, my friend Stephen picks me up, and I stroll home across charming Stuyvesant Square on my own two legs.

Cheap poetry abounds. Everything is intensely clear, shot through with a cold blue light. Clean and perfect. I am over-whelmed by a sense of bullet-dodging gratitude and an arro-gant regard for my own efficiency. My hand and arm are still on fire, but that's postsurgical. I can look forward to the day, very soon, when I will be pain free, now fully a year in the wait-ing. For now, how beautiful the world seems, how lovely the friends who deliver a potted amaryllis to my house. It blooms into a three-flowered stalk, its pink-and-white-striped petals like a child's drawing of an ideal flower, if children could actually draw. It is huge and unabashedly happy, and when that withers, *another* stalk rises up to take its place, this one with *four* exu-berant peppermint trumpets. It's like some candy-striped (and candy-assed) metaphor about the enduring power of love one might find on the side of a bottle of peach-scented body lotion, a platitude for a douche box.

Everything bustles with can-do energy. A week after surgery, the pathology report as yet undelivered, I do a reading to benefit the library of a primary school. On the bill with me are two women who read cancer-related pieces, both essentially comic in nature. One is hilarious and the other one does that annoying thing about correlating laughter and attitude with morbidity, which the psychologist James Pennebaker showed was a false connection. A sense of humor and the strength to wear sky-high Jimmy Choos to chemo is a fine stance if it works for you, but its inverse seems to constitute a failure of character, ultimately a judgment against those folks who just aren't funny or stylish enough to disarm their metastases with well-dressed wit. I am happy not to be reading *my* funny cancer story. I wear a jaunty scarf to cover the blackened, bloodstained Steri-Strips on my recently excavated neck.

About one week after that I act in a friend's short film. I wear another jaunty scarf, although the wound would hardly be out of place given my character's extended monologue: a jaded diatribe about the inevitability of death, the anarchy of the universe and its pure, unfathomable apathy for our little hopes and dreams, all delivered while smoking fake cigarettes. "Somewhere, someone is dying every second, and in the most hideous, least photogenic manner imaginable. In every hospital at every second of every day, someone is just giving up the ghost in some vile, farting, shitting, vomiting display. Every orifice discharging all at once. Their one final thought, which should be some profound, *Oh, so that's what it is,* is more often than not, I guarantee you, a simple *No! I have so many regrets! . . .*" Even as I do take after take, a small voice inside me tells me I am tempting fate with this undergraduate world-weary posturing—that, in fact, I wrote myself—that it could bite me on the ass.

———

It bites me on the ass.

I know before they even tell me that the mass is malignant. I get very quiet. I think a lot about my folks and what is going to be their third time in the role of cancer parent. I think about the ineffectual superstition in the gesture that had me inscribing books and baking cookies and delivering them here to these offices less than thirty-six hours postsurgery, as though to ensure the benign status of the tumor. Pathetic, really.

Gone is the brilliant blue light of icy purity and minty fresh health. Just like that, it's a cold winter in New York and I am back in the world of the sick, a hoosegow I really didn't think I'd see the inside of again before age sixty or so. More than twenty years prior, newly back in the city, post-lymphoma and getting on with my life, I went every Wednesday morning before work to the local public school in downtown Brooklyn to tutor a little girl in reading. The children, first and second graders, were debilitatingly cute. It embarrassed me how sweet I found them, especially one little boy whose hair was a regular cockscomb because he didn't know enough to run his hand over his head to lay it flat. At other times, he still sported a milk mustache from breakfast, or would take off his sweater which caused his T-shirt to ride up over his cherub's stomach and, like the hair, he lacked the awareness or need to pull it down for the whole morning.

The mother who coordinated the tutors was probably all of thirty-five. A Brooklyn Mom before the term meant someone with a full brownstone and a high-powered job, the off-hours from which were spent running triathlons and militant locavoraciousness culminating in butchering hogs and curing her own charcuterie. She showed up in the mornings, having gotten her kids out the door to school, hair a mess, her own shower something that could wait until she got back home midmorning. Somehow it came up that I had recently been ill, and she piped up with a cheery, "Oh, I have ovarian cancer!"

There is little in this world that I find more galvanizing than someone else in trouble. I am well aware of how dubious that sounds, coming from someone who makes a living writing in the first person. I am the furthest thing from a do-gooder. I am venal and glib and too clever by half, I know, but the thrill of the most brilliantly quicksilver aperçu is no match for the self-interested high I get from having done someone a good turn. You'd think I'd do more good turns as a result, but there you go.

Brooklyn Mom and I spoke often and openly about her illness. I remember feeling grateful that the only people around us were children, not because adults who could understand us might be traumatized by the dire nature of our conversation but because the kids' largely uninterested ears meant that she would not blow my cover. I was not happy being dragged back and reminded. It was like being away for junior year, having finally perfected an English accent, only to be visited by someone from back home who would remind me and all assembled that I was in no way British. Plus, I was too freshly out of the woods to feel safe, as if merely talking about it might bump me out of remission.

By dint of her age, or courage, or the fact that she had to try and stay alive for her children, Brooklyn Mom was confronting her illness and getting her hands dirty with it in ways I simply had not managed. She was seeking alternative treatments along with her chemo, meditating, doing regular psychotherapy, eating a macrobiotic diet, and staring her mortality in the face in a way that made me uneasy. One morning, having had a less-than-optimal result on a test, she told me about sitting at her kitchen table, eating a bowl of brown rice with the sun streaming in and illuminating everything in a warm glow. She felt such gratitude then. The world had seemed so beautiful.

In the movie *The Other Side of the Mountain,* a marvelous tearjerker biopic from my childhood, the skier Jill Kinmont severs her spinal cord on the slopes and spends the rest of her life in a wheelchair. Early on in her rehabilitation, she is visited in the hospital by her boyfriend, an impossibly handsome and fit skier. Showing off, Jill demonstrates her progress by jamming her fist into a bowl of potato chips, eventually lifting her hand to reveal one lone shard grasped tentatively between the knuckles of two crabbed fingers. "It's the hardest trick," she tells him. He is, naturally, aghast at the limited mobility and the bleakness of her life, and never visits again. (Beau Bridges will eventually step in as the amorous hero before he himself goes down in a plane something like two days before their wedding. See it. You'll cry from beginning to end, especially if you're ten and gay.)

All I could think was: *A bowl of rice? Beautiful? What kind of impoverished existence are you settling for, lady?* Brooklyn Mom was right, of course, and I would eventually get there decades later, but at that moment I could only be Jill Kinmont's shitty boyfriend, and I couldn't get out of there fast enough. In the end, my full-time secretarial job didn't allow for mornings off to tutor kids, but I was grateful for the out.

The diagnosis carries with it not a sense of relief, really—although there is a bit of a sigh after being in such terrible pain for so long, as if the long-awaited rain has finally arrived after months of threatening skies—so much as a kind of egocentric "of course." It fits with an inarticulate but ever-present sense that I have done something wrong; an infraction, inadvertent but inescapable and deep as oak roots, marring my permanent record, permanently. The piper would have to be paid. I'd say I had a grandiose sainted martyr complex, and I would be right, but in my defense, I didn't make it up out of whole cloth. I had some critical, early help. My two favorite stories as a child were Hans Christian Andersen's "The Girl Who Trod on the Loaf" and "The Happy Prince" by Oscar Wilde. I loved them both like the bitterest candy. Odd favorites for a Jewish boy, perhaps, given their intense Christian imagery, but both tales had the abstemiousness, the penance, and the ultimate sacrifice (let's just call it death, shall we?) that fed an appetite already there. What choice did I have, really? I tell you the stories here briefly, because they say so much, and because they are magnificent.

Young Inge was a beautiful and cruel child. Her physical loveliness only amplified her wickedness. She liked to pull the wings off of flies.

A poor girl, Inge is sent into service to a wealthy family who treat her well and one day send her back to her village to see her mother. On approaching the town gates, however, she spies the poor woman resting with a large bundle of kindling at her feet. Hot with shame, Inge turns back before she is even seen, her only feelings anger and contempt for such a lumpen, destitute parent.

(So far, it's *Imitation of Life,* but wait . . .)

Sometime later, Inge's mistress suggests a visit home once more, this time pressing upon the girl a large loaf of bread for her mother, which will surely be welcome. Bearing her gift, Inge sets off, proudly wearing a new cloak and a fine pair of leather shoes, picking her way over the damp ground to keep them dry and clean. Coming upon a particularly boggy stretch, Inge throws the loaf into the puddle to use it as a stepping-stone.

Such open disdain for the staff of life would not sit well in Lutheran Scandinavia, obviously, so Andersen has the loaf sink underground, with Inge on it, beneath the mud into the brewery of the Marsh Woman. "A cesspool is a wonderful palace compared with the Marsh Woman's brewery. Every vessel is reeking with horrible smells that would turn a human being faint, and they are packed closely together; but even if there were enough space between them to creep through, it would be impossible because of the slimy toads and the fat snakes that are creeping and slithering along." It is here that Inge spends an age, fused to her bread, frozen with the cold and unable to move. But this is just a stop on her downward journey, because one day Satan himself visits, along with his great-grandmother—who is, not surprisingly, a total fucking bitch. It is decided that the frozen Inge would make a pleasing addition to her antechamber, and so the girl is taken down to Hell itself. There she stands, moving only her eyes, witness to the countless torments of the souls around her, her once lovely clothes filthy and enslimed, covered in toads, twined with snakes, foul, debased.

And *still* she is unrepentant! "This is what comes of trying to have clean feet," she says, consoling herself that everyone is looking at her with envy. Even so, such attention cannot stop her from being overwhelmed with a hunger that seems to eat her very insides. She wonders if she can stand it much longer, but endure it she must. For much, much longer.

Up above, life goes on without her, but she is not forgotten. The hot tears of her mother splash down upon her forehead, to no avail. "A mother's tears of grief for her erring child always reach it, but they do not redeem; they only burn, and they make the pain greater." (Let it never be said that the Jews have cornered the market on maternal guilt.) Her employers remember her as a sinful girl. "She did not value the gifts of our Lord, but trampled them underfoot. It will be hard for her to have the gates of mercy opened to let her in."

Like many a fallen woman, Inge becomes a cautionary tale. Children are put to sleep with her story; they jump rope, keeping time with chants about her ignominious and richly deserved fall from grace. Only one little girl expresses sympathy for Inge. Eight decades later, this same little girl, now an old woman on her deathbed, once more sheds a tear for Inge, the scalding, purifying drop reaching all the way down to Hades to burn the forehead of the wretch, who is instantly resurrected as the most modest and abstemious of timid brown sparrows. Cowering in doorways, Sparrow Inge takes only the barest sustenance for herself from the crumbs she gathers, giving the rest away to other birds. Finally, after she has given away crumbs equal in volume and mass to the loaf she had defiled with her selfishness, only then is she taken up to heaven to serve at His feet.

The Happy Prince is a gilded, jewel-encrusted statue, a brilliantly shining colossus standing proudly above a harbor town. One autumn evening, a swallow flying south decides to stop overnight before continuing to Egypt to meet his friends. Nestling himself comfortably between the Prince's feet, he is disturbed by a raindrop on his head, although the sky is clear. Looking up, he sees that it is the statue crying.

In life, it seems, the prince had lived a beautiful and sequestered existence behind the walled gardens of the palace of Sans Souci. But now, seeing all the human suffering below him, the Happy Prince cannot help but weep, even though his statue heart is made of lead. ("'What, is he not solid gold?' said the Swallow to himself. He was too polite to make any personal remarks out loud." Wilde interjects, unable to resist.)

The prince entreats the swallow to pluck the ruby from his sword hilt and fly with it to the poor home of a haggard seamstress whose child is ill. The swallow does so and fans the feverish boy's head with his wings, sending the sick child into delicious slumber.

The next day, with the cold incrementally creeping in, the swallow bids goodbye to the prince and makes ready for his flight to Egypt, but the prince begs him to stay just one more night, and to pluck out one of his sapphire eyes and take it down to a destitute playwright, too distracted by the cold to write in his chilly garret.

Same drill the next day. Much colder, and another thwarted sayonara as the prince implores the swallow to pluck out the other sapphire and deliver it to a little match girl (Wilde cribbing his archetype of abjection from Mr. Andersen).

His jeweled eyes gone, the prince is blind now, and the swallow vows to never leave his side, encroaching winter be damned. The swallow tells of all the suffering he sees in his flights over the town, and slowly denudes the statue of its gold leaf and distributes the valuable wafers among the poor.

Fully winter now, the statue is dull and the swallow a goner. With one last kiss upon the prince's once-rosebud mouth, the bird falls dead at his feet, the gentle thump of his tiny, flightless body followed by a muffled crack, the sound of the prince's lead heart breaking in two. Both carcasses are thrown upon the town rubbish heap.

The story ends with God dispatching his angels to earth to bring back the two most precious items in Christendom. The dead bird and cracked heart are brought to heaven, presumably to spend eternity in a paradise of self-denial alongside the little Sparrow Inge.

Is it any wonder, then, that I should feel destined for great things? (And by great, of course, I mean terrible.)

Dr. X looks a good deal older than his Web photo; he is a man over seventy. He finds me in a consulting room. "Mr. Sauer?" he asks, beckoning me into his office. "No, Rakoff," I correct him. I smile at my sister, who has come down from Toronto for the meeting. We've still not told my parents, who are abroad. I don't want to ruin their trip, especially if all that is required is another minor surgery.

Dr. X continues for a good few minutes wondering aloud who Sauer is, offering me some of his onion bialy, asking me once more if I'm *sure* I'm not Mr. Sauer, insisting that I really ought to take some bialy, and suddenly remembering Sauer. I like mildly eccentric people and Dr. X has a certain cantankerous New York Jewish sensibility I've always enjoyed. What does become a little frustrating is the almost thirty minutes he spends talking to me, while my scans and pathology slides sit on his secretary's desk not fifteen feet away and he makes no move to get up and examine them. When he finally does, the news is not good. My malignant peripheral nerve sheath sarcoma, high grade—not quite as amusingly Navajo-Yiddish sounding—was likely caused by the radiation I received for my first bout of cancer at age twenty-two. The margins are not clean. He shows me in the microscope, which frankly interests me only marginally. It is the Friday before Christmas. He wants me to come in on Monday to be fitted with a port, so that on Tuesday I might begin a double dose of chemotherapy, "a rough course," he assures me, all leading up to the main event in three months' time, the complete amputation of my left arm. Only surgery will tell if there will be enough cancer-free shoulder or collarbone to preserve some sense of thoracic symmetry for the attachment of a cosmesis (the only-for-show, functionless cousin of a prosthesis). I get mildly weepy in the waiting room when I think that I will predecease the parents, something I emphatically do not want to do. I have a CAT scan of my neck and chest, and some blood work, but Dr. X leaves before looking at the results. Still, I feel safe in his hands. I might even love him a little, this third physician in three weeks upon whom I have bestowed all my hopes.

My sister, cousin, and I go for clam chowder (establishing once and for all that there is essentially nothing in the world that can put me off my food). My sister and I call the parents that midnight, early morning where they are visiting. We ruin their holiday and then go to bed. I will say this only once, but I will mean it thousands of times, and with all, *all* of my heart: thank you, you various alcohols, benzodiazepines, and codeine derivatives. I love you all very, very much.

They say there are no atheists in foxholes, and while there are not words to convey how little I want to lose my arm, I am still not moved to either pray or ask "Why me?" I am angry that I ever got the radiation for my Hodgkin's back in 1987, although if it's anybody's fault, it is mine. It had been presented to me as an easier option than chemotherapy. Less comprehensive but also less toxic, no vomiting, for example. I opted for the radiation out of fear of the more difficult but more pervasively effective alternative. Dave the Brave had proven himself unworthy of even his cheap medal and made the easy decision, rather than embracing the fear and the rigor of the strenuous life. In the end, the radiation didn't even work, and I had to have the chemo anyway. There is little I can do about it now. I try to take comfort in remembering David Lykken's twins study: *They'll take my arm off in March, and six months after that, I'll be back to my old self. By September I will be fine.* I say this over and over again. (I do, however, want to call up the acupuncturist and say, "Hey, Einstein! Hey, genius! Remember that *wind* in my arm?")

The parents arrive and take the bed and I join my sister on the pullout couch. The median age in the apartment is now sixty, which is also the approximate number of square feet per person. Things are looking up, actually. In the intervening two days since I saw him, Dr. X has been discredited by no fewer than three other oncologists I speak to. One diplomatically states that "He gets amazing results that cannot be duplicated," which is essentially calling him a fraud, although it's not nearly as damning as a former colleague of his who simply screams an alarmed "NO! You must not be treated by this man!" when he hears X's name. My heroic friend Kent gets us in to see a sarcoma specialist at Sloan-Kettering, the world-famous cancer hospital that sponsors the public radio morning broadcast, and where they've seen more of this quite rare cancer (ain't I special) than anywhere else in the country. Kent assuages my fears by pointing out that Sloan is very conservative in its approach to amputations, only performing them in the most extreme cases. In the meantime, my mother the physician has worked her extensive Toronto connections and I will also fly up for a second opinion at the cancer hospital where I was treated twenty-two years previously.

I cook a Christmas Eve dinner for eight, but it's really a second Thanksgiving, the army of friends who have mobilized in my behalf, and the restored and continued attachment of my left arm chief among the things for which I am grateful, ambidextrous huzzahs all around. *How silly to have ever thought to trust a dangerous quack like evil, stupid, fucking Dr. X,* I chide myself. My medical crush officially over, my too-freely-given transference is rescinded and I wait, dance card and pencil in hand, ready to jot down the name of my next savior.

My sister leaves on Christmas Day to be with her family. My parents leave the following morning. I put them in a cab and go directly to the gym. In general, there is no colder, no more clinical nor honest referendum on one's desirability than the gym, specifically the steam room at the gym. One's powers of conversation, one's wit, books one might have written, even one's pretty eyes won't get you very far. But lo, behold three randy Magi, bearing not frankincense or myrrh, nor gold but for a thin chain on one of them, with little more than towels (and barely towels, at that), and yet with these humble gifts do we provide one another succor, diversion, release. Verily, we are risen. It is a Boxing Day miracle.

The very nice radiation oncologist lays his warm hands on my neck and collarbone and talks in his warm Irish voice about the treatments: five weeks or so, followed by surgery to remove whatever tumor is still there. I can do it up here in Toronto or down in New York, which would be my preference. It's only at the moment before he's about to send in the surgeon that he says, "Now *he* might say something completely different," that I get that old twinge of antecedent-phrase-leading-up-to-an-as-yet-unspoken-but-inevitably-hope-dashing bombshell, like "I think you have a future in film," or "You're a great guy, David, who deserves love." *A-ha,* I think in anticipation.

A-ha indeed. The CAT scan seems to reveal a fairly significant amount of tumor still there, one that looks like it's wrapped around the major nerves and blood vessels of the arm. This is no longer crazy Dr. X talking. When an expert who is not a psychotic charlatan goes out on a limb (*har de har har*) to even mention such a thing, he's essentially telling you it's a fait accompli. My arm is back on the table, so to speak.

My mother is shaking a little, but only in the hands. We thank the doctors. They leave. We put our coats back on and embrace briefly, both dry-eyed. "Rough sledding, Davey," she says. If I have ever shown any stoicism in my life, I know where it comes from.

And down the rough hill we sled. I am back to trying to be unsentimental about a nondominant limb, doing the trade-off in my mind: an arm for continued existence. It's an exchange I can live with, although I am fixated on how radical the cut: from neck to armpit, leaving me without even a shoulder to balance things out. I imagine that the rest of my life I will see the tiniest involuntary flinching on the faces of people as they react with an immediate and preconscious disgust at the asymmetry of my silhouette. Nevertheless, I become Julie Norem's little foot soldier, defensive pessimism in action, puncturing my fear by learning to go without something before it's officially discontinued; weaning myself off of saffron or Iranian caviar before it becomes no longer available, and trying to ascribe a similar luxurious dispensability to my left arm. I begin to type with one hand. (One finger is more like it. Considering what I do for a living, it's appalling that I'm still hunt-and-peck.) I accomplish a host of tasks: putting on my shoes (new slip-ons purchased without even looking at the price tag. I remember this kind of heedless spending in the face of illness), buttoning my fly, showering, dressing, shaving. I manage to cut an avocado in half by wedging the leathery black pear against the counter with my stomach and, thus steadied, go at it with a knife. In the evenings, with my bloodstream a sticky river of Ativan, wine, and codeine, it all feels eminently doable. In the cold light of day, however, unable to carry a chair to move it into a corner, for example, what I'm about to embark on feels a little bigger and harder.

There are other extra-functional and non-cosmetic realities I have to consider. How does someone without a left arm know he's having a heart attack, for example? And the sarcoma, for reasons they don't know—or can't stop, anyway—has a one-third to one-half chance of reappearing in my lungs. If it's something small they can excise, great, but it might also appear as a bloom of lesions for which they can prescribe aggressive chemo, but it doesn't really work, and that would be that, I'm afraid. Such thoughts, which I try to keep at bay, build to a momentum that inevitably leads to the conviction that the metastases are already under way; that, like it or not, just like that film monologue stated, this is exactly how people die; the cemeteries are crowded with indispensable men, those younger, more beautiful, more deserving of futures than I, multitudes of people who were more full of life (until, I suppose, they weren't), who had parents more adoring. A few years back, I knew and said goodbye to scores of young men who died criminally before their time, and certainly it was not because they wanted to live less than I do. Barack Obama's grandmother, for heaven's sake, a woman who essentially raised him, died mere days before he was elected. Surely she would have lingered to see him become the most powerful person in the free world if she could have. It gives the lie to those well-worn anecdotes of people managing to hold on to see daughters married or grandchildren born. There will be little I can do about it, ultimately.

I try to comfort myself with the first-person accounts I've heard of those who die on operating tables and come back: the light, the warmth, and the surge of love from one's dead ancestors urging you forward. But even that doesn't help as I wonder what on earth the Old World, necromancing Litvak primitives from whom I am descended would make of me? *You're forty-four and not married? You're a what? We had one in the shtetl and he was chased from the town with brickbats.* How much *treyf* do you eat? *What kind of writing? And from this you make a living?*

This does not help. Neither does contemplating the fact that my surrounding physical world will have a similar paucity of beauty in concert with my soon-to-be monstrous form. I have, in the past, inveighed against those whose aesthetic tyranny made them have only three perfect teacups in their home, say. What happens when one has four people to tea? Now, at the threshold of becoming dependent on gadgetry from low-tech button hooks to strange cyborgian hydraulics, should they become available, all my principled outrage comes tumbling down. I think of all the devices that will govern my future life, a host of tools encroaching on my elegant and lovely apartment, all of them rendered in functional plastic in that super-ugly shade of almond, the universal hue of therapeutic aid.

I can recall seeing many un-legged souls, but armless fellows, far fewer. I have a vague memory of a white-haired war veteran, the empty sleeve of his suit jacket tucked inside the pocket. He is wearing a medal-festooned beret along with a red felt poppy pinned to his lapel, standing at one of the many parades in honor of those who fell in the Great War, an event of annual frequency in my Anglo Canadian youth. Will I manage a similar elegance and dignity, I wonder? It's doubtful. An old quip springs to mind about people who used to marvel at the remarkable spryness of the aged Katharine Hepburn, saying, "I hope *I* look that good when I'm ninety." To which one need only point out that, unless one was a marble-featured, lithe beauty who looked like her in *The Philadelphia Story* now, the odds were slim to none.

I fly back to New York to see more doctors and get the apartment ready for one-armed living, although I haven't a clue what that means. Airport security is a scary affair in what it bodes. The simple act of discarding the metal from my pockets has me panic that I am holding folks up. I cheat and use my left arm for the first time in days. Undoubtedly there will be special lines for people like me, but I can't get rid of the dark visions of being victimized. Not by society or anything of that nature. (I promise not to feel alienated when fashion spreads in magazines refuse to run photos of amputees. I already feel sufficiently distant and ignored by the world and concerns of models.) I mean literally victimized, targeted as an easy mark, rolled, mugged, or worse. And I confess that some of these grimmer scenarios involve people of low degree, who I will have invited into my home myself. I can't really envision a future where anything resembling consensual physical contact is in the cards. Whatever sex I have from here on out will most probably have to be purchased. With my days as an eligible bachelor or anything remotely resembling a catch almost up, it's now entirely too late for me to hoodwink someone into sticking around for the horror show.

The dream is fairly classic, by which I mean, utterly banal. I have somehow pissed off a mobster by not watching my mouth and letting loose some bit of unchecked criticism. I am bundled into his car, where I begin sucking up in my fear, even as I loathe myself for my cowardice. He starts telling me about his

215

estate somewhere near Palm Beach, or France, where he does his big-game hunting, and I'm in his car the whole time, conversing, shucking, jiving, drawing him out sycophantically to distract him. As we approach my apartment, it's clear that I'm not simply going to be allowed out of the vehicle. I must pay a price for my words: a short wooden stake plunged directly through my (yawn) left hand. It will be a mark of my betrayal. "Please," I say. "I'll blow you!" I offer desperately. He's a very ugly man. There is only desperation and not a trace of the erotic in this gesture. "Ah, I don't like blow jobs, really," he replies. (As a child at a picnic, rocking a hula hoop or something, another child came up to me asking to use it. "I'll be your best friend," he entreated. "Best friend?" I said, all of seven years old but already a prig in the making. "I hardly *know* you.") I am desperate not to be stabbed. "Stop being so anxious about it, and it will be much easier," he says.

A friend asks if I've "picked out" my prosthetic yet, as though I'd have my choice of titanium-plated cyborgiana at my disposal, like some amputee Second Life World of Warcraft character. Another friend, upon hearing my news, utters an unedited, "Oh my God, that's so depressing!" Over supper, I am asked by another, "So if it goes to the lungs, is it all over?" Regrettably very possibly, I reply, and when I go on to mention as how they no longer give much radiation for Hodgkin's, he says, "Well, you got twenty-five years out of it," as if the radiation was a defenseless washing machine I was maligning, and what did I expect, really?

But here's the point I want to make about the stuff people say. Unless someone looks you in the eye and hisses, "You fucking asshole, I can't *wait* until you die of this," people are really trying their best. Just like being happy and sad, you will find yourself on both sides of the equation many times over your lifetime, either saying or hearing the wrong thing. Let's all give each other a pass, shall we?

I go to a production of *Our Town*. The play about the inhabitants of Grover's Corners at the turn of the century is moving in its simplicity. With the exception of maybe a bowl of string beans, all the props are mimed. The costumes are minimal and not period in any way. In the last act, Emily, now dead, begs to return for just one more day among the living. Her wish granted, she leaves her grave—a folding chair—and pulls aside a curtain, and behind it, there is Life! A fully decorated set of her childhood home's kitchen, with frost on the windows and a sink with a pump that works and her mother, young again and now in 1900s dress making breakfast on an actual stove. Such sound and activity, it is almost too much joy, too much physical presence for both Emily and us. And then, the director David Cromer's brilliant coup: the smell of the bacon that is really cooking slowly reaches us all in the audience. That great, domestic olfactory "Yes!" (except for the pigs, for whom it's a "no" about as definitive as they come), and I want it all: I want the bacon and all it entails, I want my arm, but even more than that, I want the years. I cry. It is my Susan Hayward moment.

My mother calls with potentially good news. The most recent MRI might have shown that the arm doesn't need to be taken. *Keep your powder dry*, I think. I continue to do most things one-handed. Returning too soon to the world of ambidexterity would show ingratitude for my gifts. It would be tantamount to stepping on the loaf of bread to protect my pretty shoes.

I meet the surgeon, Carol Morris. An elegant and calming presence, she's like a cross between Sigourney Weaver and Michelle Obama. When she finally says, "I don't see a need for amputation," I burst into tears. It seems I'm racking up the Susan Hayward moments.

And so: five weeks of radiation to sterilize and cauterize the remaining tumor, and then surgery, the hope being that they can get it all this time. They will, however, have to sever some nerves to get it out. I won't be able to use my triceps. If I lift my arm over my shoulder, it will flop back down onto my head. Again, I welcome the thought of years of being smacked in the face by my own left hand.

The first week of radiation is almost euphoric. Such an exciting task ahead of me. It's the scene where the teacher comes to the small village. The children, sleek-limbed and beautiful, in pressed white shirts, stand in formation in front of the one-room school that will also serve as the teacher's new home. They sing a song of welcome and all seems absolutely right and bursting with promise.

To wit: the rosy sunrises that greet me each morning as I walk out at 6:45 to get the bus on First Avenue. And then, as we reach Thirty-seventh Street, to our right the East River and the big sky above it opens up in an expanse of newest day. And how lucky that, here it is, February, and not really so cold as all that, and the handy Purell dispensers everywhere in the hospital that dribble out palmfuls of the disinfectant with an automatic salivary whir, just by putting your hand under them, will keep me healthy and antiseptic. Plus, free graham crackers on every floor. Everyone in the hospital is so unbelievably kind that just going is therapeutic in and of itself. I start to regret what I've done with my life, seriously calculating whether, if I manage to beat this, I could make a change and enter one of the helping professions. I sound like the narrator of *Bleak House,* a female of such treacly aspect that, as I vaguely remember, she almost cries out with delight when she contracts smallpox. Oh, what marvelous life lessons she'll learn, what a curative to the venality and sin that were surely festering just behind her unmarred visage. So what if there is an interval most every morning when the wide plate of the radiation machine positions itself directly in front of my face—like some curious and possibly hungry predator, studying me dispassionately as its scrim of lead rods reassemble themselves, leaving a gap that resembles California through which the radiation will pass and penetrate my neck—and my heart starts to beat like a panicked bird in a rapidly heating cage. And who cares if that leads my thoughts to turn yet again to my lungs, invaded, Jackson Pollocked with cancer like a spatter pattern in a crime scene. Just listen to the Billie Holiday CD I brought in, recite the Elizabeth Bishop: *In your next letter I wish you'd say / where you are going and what you are doing* . . . Get through it.

And it remains eminently manageable, even as it gets harder to run to the bus stop in the morning. That scene of school-in-the-village perfection is starting to show some cracks as the weeks go on. A perplexing rustling in the thatch of my roof. When I ask one of my students about it, he says the local word for cockroach, and then places his thumb and forefinger an uncomfortably long distance apart to indicate the size of the critters. Oh well, no bother yet. Ever gaily forward, slather on the greasy moisturizer to protect your radiated skin, realize that no one can really give you the assurance that you will beat this thing, no matter how many times you ask them. Pay no mind to the older brother of one of your students who starts to show up every day and stands at the back of the classroom wearing army fatigues and holding a machine gun.

It is something of a comfort not to feel like one is twisting in the wind alone. Julie Norem's age of discontent seems to have dawned. Most everyone I know is having trouble, some fuzziness that blurs the borders between the micro and the macro, momentarily conflating their own personal problems and the global economic meltdown. It seems to all of us that the center is not holding anywhere, everything is prone to breakdown, entropy, the world feels lethally friable. The best-laid plans, one's most fastidious contingency strategies have revealed themselves in the cold light of day to be laughably inadequate, no match for the happenstance that seems of late only to promise death, mayhem, poverty, flood. And here you are, having spent all that time protecting your home from the oncoming elements only to find that it has been shored up with crackers.

I might be the cutest patient on the floor, a dubious honor on a cancer ward. Not so the results of my surgery, which are an unambiguous gold medal. Dr. Morris was able to peel the entire tumor away. It went better than even she had hoped. I will have use of my triceps, and as for the margins, "They're clean but close," she says. Cancer is pass-fail. I'll take it.

I stay four days in the hospital, two of which are challenged by my (generally very good, paid for out of pocket) insurance company, their official reasoning being that I could hobble to the toilet and take my pain meds by mouth, as if I was some robust malingerer or had checked myself in for a boob job. We appeal. We win. But may I briefly say . . . *what the fuck?* I paid my hefty premiums, even as I ran out of money due to my unproductive year-plus of pain, plus hospital bills. But I am lucky in my background and prospects, my connections that allow me to marshal, at a moment's notice, three oncologists to save my arm, or another dear friend who is an attorney to challenge the insurance company. All of it means that I remained essentially affluent despite a near-zero bank balance. How are people supposed to manage? How did elected officials have the balls to even try to spin their wrong-side-of-history bullshit as being in our interests? Or moral? It is the duty of society to take care of its individuals, plain and simple. We will never be healthier than our sickest member.

In Trader Joe's, not two hours post-discharge from the hospital, in a coincidence to make even the most melodramatic fiction-workshop hack throw up his hands and say "Oh, *come* on!," I walk by a guy with no left arm or shoulder. I swear it. Everything but a sandwich board saying "There but for the grace of God . . ." From my safe vantage, I can say he doesn't look half bad.

I am still in pain, two months later. A chatty e-mail takes it out of my arm and exhausts me. I am unproductive, which embarrasses me. At a birthday party, a nice young woman in a Marimekko-ish dress tells me about her book proposal and her project sounds so smart and erudite that I can only hear it as an indictment of myself and my sloth. Only the next morning do I remember that this is what I felt two decades prior when I moved back to New York post-treatment, having been out of the slipstream for eighteen months and feeling hopelessly behind the curve. I would be out delivering a package—one of the necessary humiliations of assistant-hood in the book trade—and would see acquaintances from college up ahead and start announcing from a distance of twenty feet away to people I barely knew and shouldn't have cared about, "I'm not a messenger!"

After a year and a half, I am a connoisseur of unpleasant physical sensation. All the subtleties of my pain and its gradations become quite clear. Sometimes its onset is stealthy but definitive, like having one's boat gently ease up onto a sandbar with a gentle, granular squeak and there you are, stuck. I take something, and after a while, close to an hour as I sit there in my run-aground vessel, the water level gradually rises until my skiff is lifted and I am afloat once more.

At other times, the pain comes on like the various instruments of a jazz combo in the wee small hours. The surgical site starts the riff with a slow but steady rhythm—cymbals caressed with brushes—joined shortly thereafter by the piano pulsations of my thumb and forefinger, the old standbys who began it all. Finally things get into full swing with the lead melody of the triceps, a forceful trumpet. Once the song has begun in earnest and I've sat through a few choruses, I head to the pill bottle to take one (vainly wishing I could follow the implicit advice of Dave Brubeck and actually take five). My analgesics of choice are Percocet and OxyContin, the latter apparently the stuff the kids in middle America are ruining their lives over, albeit by crushing it up and snorting it. In the absence of discomfort, and taken so heedlessly, it must be wonderful, but all it really does is take me from negative five to zero, and that's enough. Perhaps these OxyContin kids are young positive psychologists in the making, staking out their right to go from zero to positive five.

Despite this Inuit-fifty-words-for-snow taxonomy of pain's manifold forms, I cannot fashion a dwelling from frozen blocks of it, or cunningly use a thinly falling curtain of it to conceal my form while hunting seal. The most I can glean from it is a siren call to seek pharmaceutical attention, and I got that message a while back.

I have been asked a few times if I've learned anything. It's not a chastising question, the way one might interrogate a tearful four-year-old after releasing him from his time-out in the corner, and I don't know that I have the answer. This isn't my first time at the rodeo. I've already faced mortality and my body's rather startling lack of allegiance once before, but was I perhaps in need of some cosmic corrective of my venal ways? Did I need to be rendered more thankful, less cavalier, less glib, maybe? Again, I've tried to be all of those things, although whether I've been successful is not for me to say.

After a lot of urging myself and others to regard terrible outcomes unflinchingly, to *really think* on such matters and championing those among us who cannot help but do so, it turns out that, with the wolf just outside my open windows—closer at hand than I really feared he would ever get to me at this age, with his hot breath bothering the curtains—I'd rather not dwell on it, which is kind of funny, if you think about it.

As for the fear that has marked a lot of this, it is bereft of larger lessons. Other than the reflexive survival instincts it triggers, avoiding being something else's dinner, it seems completely useless. I don't mean that as a macho preamble to the phrase "so I choose not to feel it and just go on as if I didn't." I mean that fear lays waste to one's best reserves. It foments rot in my stores of grain, eats away at my timbers. If I dwell on the possibility that I might be dead by forty-seven, I can't really find a useful *therefore* in that. Therefore I will train for the marathon, confess the long-unspoken torch carried for X, etc. I once joked

223

that if I knew the world would end in one day, I'd probably just break into a bakery and eat all the éclairs I wanted. But true fear—which, luck of the draw, doesn't ambush me as much as it might or as much as I'd thought it would—just leaves me frozen; amotivated and stunned. Dinner, in an evolutionary word.

I have scans at the three-month mark. My lungs remain unchanged, thank goodness. As for the surgical site, they see a lot of changes, but are fairly comfortable in deeming it postoperative inflammation. *Fairly* comfortable. They will watch it closely and send me for an MRI in another three months, and another scan three months thereafter. And so begins my life for the next five to ten years, if I'm lucky. There is just a baseline uncertainty that will need to be lived with. I finally understand what Julie Norem meant when she told me that one could be simultaneously anxious and happy. The assurances are momentary, at best half comforting, like being told "That's not a man in your room. It's just your clothes draped over the back of a chair casting a shadow, see? However, there *is* actually an insane, knife-wielding murderer loose in the neighborhood. G'night."

Everybody's got something. In the end, what choice does one really have but to understand that truth, to really take it in, and then shop for groceries, get a haircut, do one's work; get on with the business of one's life.

That's the hope, anyway.

DON'T GET TOO COMFORTABLE

David Rakoff takes us on a bitingly funny grand tour of our culture of excess. Whether he is contrasting the elegance of one of the last flights of the supersonic Concorde with the good-times-and-chicken-wings populism of Hooters Air, working as a cabana boy at a South Beach hotel, or traveling to a private island off the coast of Belize to watch a soft-core video shoot—where he is provided with his very own personal manservant—rarely have greed, vanity, selfishness, and vapidity been so mercilessly skewered. Simultaneously a Wildean satire and a plea for a little human decency, *Don't Get Too Comfortable* shows that far from being bobos in paradise, we're in a special circle of gilded-age hell.

Social Science/Essays

FRAUD

From *This American Life* alum David Rakoff comes a hilarious collection that single-handedly raises self-deprecation to an art form. Whether impersonating Sigmund Freud in a department store window during the holidays, climbing an icy mountain in cheap loafers, or learning primitive survival skills in the wilds of New Jersey, Rakoff clearly demonstrates how he doesn't belong—nor does he try to. In his debut collection of essays, Rakoff uses his razor-sharp wit and snarky humor to deliver a barrage of damaging blows that, more often than not, land squarely on his own jaw—hilariously satirizing the writer, not the subject. Joining the wry and the heartfelt, *Fraud* offers an object lesson in not taking life, or ourselves, too seriously.

Humor/Essays

ANCHOR BOOKS
Available at your local bookstore, or visit
www.randomhouse.com